"*Prairie Hearts* makes a significant contribution to the works of women writers. Whitney Scott should be commended for exposing us to such a rich and diverse compendium of writing talent."

— *Chicago Books in Review*

Prairie Hearts

Women View the the Midwest

Edited and Designed
by
Whitney Scott

Outrider Press, Inc.
Crete, Illinois

*Book Design and Formatting
by Whitney Scott*

Library of Congress
Catalog Card Number
96-68101

Copyright 1996, Outrider Press, Inc.

ISBN 0-9621039-3-4

Outrider Press, Inc.
1004 East Steger Road, Suite C-3
Crete, Illinois
60417-1362

Acknowledgements

Thanks to Karen Darr and Terri Dousias

Table of Contents

Editor's Introduction

The Midwest is another country – a state of mind some suggest – a study in contrasts as freezing winds ice bare branches, giving way suddenly to scorching summers – a two-season country, both equally hard to bear, but each with its own beauty.

Wander deep into the fields. Admire a dozing owl, fluffy against gray streaks of winter sky. Or a red-tailed hawk riding a current high above, minutes from suburban sprawl and urban density. Or the sumptuously ornate delicacy of fruit blossoms set against the stark simplicity of a flat, flat Midwestern field ending in the far horizon without a hint of high ground in sight. Here, all is one-point perspective.

Is there a spiritual heartland lived by a few, idealized by many? There are those who say it's a popular myth sustained by media dreams. Others may find its soil fertile in unimagined ways.

It is a place of opportunity and artistic expression in urban centers, possible isolation and stagnation in its outlying areas – where some poets, writers and other artists refer to themselves as "survivors" of the region, while others in the arts flourish. It is a place of narrow tractor paths between fields and, some say, narrower minds – a place whose fields nourish not only a single, large country but many worldwide.

Certainly, many of the nationwide contributors in this collection reveal the startling contrasts in the region as they evoke the splendor of an early-morning mist catching the first sun's rays over the fields – yet draw with equal clarity characters often stunted by meager dreams and smaller opportunities, some content to remain, others yearning to explore larger, distant freedoms far from the flat land and lives they see around them.

In her celebration of the special Midwestern beauty that thrives in a land of extremes, Kathy Mayer of Lafayette, Indiana, writes tenderly in "Angela's Folly Bloomed…" of

"A thick ground cover in green and silver
its variegated leaves stay green all winter,
then pop out in puffy purple blooms for spring.
It flowers until well until November, this
optimistic, hardy plant touch with grace…"

Equally loving in a different way is the short story "I-57" by Laura Smith Porter of Worcester, Massachusetts. She paints a landscape of enduring loyalty, courage and caring between Virginia and her husband, Bud, as they face his terminal illness traveling between their home and the hospitals of Chicago.

In contrast as sharp as the outcroppings of rock in farm fields, Nancy Peiffer of Evanston, Illinois, writes scathingly

"The heartland I know has no Rockwell families
it's the home of hidden bruises
and untold stories..."

Many of those stories are, in fact, told here. Marilyn Coffey of Hays, Kansas, won the top poetry prize in *Prairie Hearts'* national contest for her stunning portrayal of the "Men of Nebraska."

"Straight-legged and tight-lipped they walk
the men on the main streets of Lincoln
Faces crease as neatly as perma-press seams
ironed by a life pursuing the rectangular
A life run as straight as their streets, as narrow:
laid out at right angles to the known earth's four corners..."

San Franciscan Stacey Thoyre's "The Flight of Mrs. Hank Wallace," winner in the fiction division, depicts a marriage so constrained by speechless rage that only a long-kept secret remains to define a widow's memory of the 37 years spent with a man whose disdainful looks silenced, withered and shrank her.

Most haunting, perhaps, is Marcia Karlin's poem, "Fallen Angels," inspired by a local Illinois newspaper report of vandals destroying several religious sculptures in a sanctuary and using a broken statue of Jesus Christ to bludgeon and blind a nesting swan there. This outstanding piece won the Outrider Press prize for the best submission by a member of the Feminist Writers Guild.

Grazina Smith of Chicago writes in a similarly tragic vein with her story of an abused wife who is "On the Road to Recovery." She must somehow be separated from her delusions about her husband, a man held in high regard by the unseeing society surrounding her.

The stories and poems in *Prairie Hearts* not only explore the contrasts of the beautiful and the ugly; many evoke the rich heritage of the Great Plains Native American tribes, providing fertile themes for a number of the writers anthologized here. Chicago's Susanna

Lang writes of the Chippewa tale in her poem, "South Manitou Island," where "...the dune's a bear who sleeps, and waits for her two cubs....two islands in the bay..." Similarly, sacred Native American burial grounds inspire Jane Haldiman of Chicago, who ponders these ancient energies in "Another visit to Cahokia Mounds."

> "The buried history's echo keeps its beat,
> a soundless cleft within the skin of Monk's Mound.
> The weeds' impatient gossip at my feet
> chafes restless currents up my legs, competes
> with wooden stairs that climb and mask the grounds..."

From Fairfax, Virginia, Gwyn McVay's images in "Hawk Season" powerfully portray the bird revered by many Native Americans, and Marcia Schwartz of Los Angeles recalls warriors' visions seen through an eagle's eye in her poem, "Celebrating the West."

Perhaps the force and spirit of the arts best bridge the gaps marking life's contrasts – in seasons, attitudes, cultures and dreams. These collected voices of a wide range of women throughout the nation affirm that belief. In Claudia Rosa Silva's "The El Tunnel," set in her native Chicago, an African's powerful music reaches a proud Latina, transcending their differences and briefly binding them together. Carol Gloor describes the transformative power of "Monet in Chicago" in the city that is home to her; Matisse's *Bathers by a River* "At the Chicago Art Institute" inspires the spare, erotically charged imagery of Massachusetts' Mary Damon Peltier, who is moved by

> "the tenderness of bellies
> vulnerable navel
> the flesh hand curves to touch
> hip that rises   comes forward
> silver-lit bone..."

These writings from women of all ages, backgrounds, ethnicities and beliefs portray the land of contrasts that is the Midwest. Truly, the heartland's geography and heritage inspiring these works make it as unforgettable as the poetry and fiction in this collection.

Whitney Scott
March, 1996

Prairie Hearts

City River by Judith Arcana

City rivers have a hard time.
People drop candy wrappers over their railings –
lit cigarettes, beer cans, dead batteries.

Can Chicago know it once was wild like McKenzie?
Forced against itself, drawn away from the great lake,
can Chicago live in its memory
of stones rounded smooth, trees leaning over
reflections in glassy pools, great birds
hovering   diving   striking
at the flash of silver in rocky shallows?

Does Chicago know it once could be *heard* –
riffling, booming, churning down its length to the lake?
Does Chicago remember that once, time before this oily green,
it was black with smooth mud, running clear
beyond the marsh?

Does it see people in the fatbottomed tourboats,
rows of metal chairs on deck, loud: "…the Merchandise Mart,
owned at one time by Joseph Kennedy…"?
Can it remember the others, who silently held the surface
in slim wooden boats painted magic?

Can Chicago wonder: did the magic people take the trees,
drop the stones inside their leather packs and walk away?
Or does the river know that they too have lost
the sky, birds, banks of earth dense with roots?

Zenith by Janet Baker

To outdo the rooster
in proclaiming dawn,
the noon whistle yowls
from the red bulb
atop the water tower
that bears the village name.

Dogs yelp in painful chorus,
spines contract,
and village life cringes.
Lunch is announced
over the dry corn dust
of the grain elevator.

It drowns the moaning doves
and squawk of jays, and
squeal of children in midair
on schoolyard swings. Then
unsurpassed, the Angelus bells
begin their mournful count. Angels
telling virgins a dozen times over
that they will bear gods.

You do not have a town
without a whistle, the village
fathers knew. The stake is
planted with a water tower,
and time is conquered with
this noontime climax and
communal howl.

Basement by Janet Baker

Cavernous rooms
Dark mirrors of the house above
Where mice scamper and
Punished children hide.

Swollen Mason jars sit on
Cobwebbed shelves in the old
Coal room, food for ghosts,
No one removes them.

Dank, blackened world suffused with
Strong detergent and bleach
Groaning of the washing machine
Moaning of my mother's songs of love.

Refuge from tornadoes
Moldy hole for huddling in fear
Our house might blow overhead.
We would watch it fly free.

Gathering place of dirty laundry
Fumes of old sweat, the family stench
Heaped in the ghastly place
We are banished for cleansing.

The Old Tree
by Donna Black

Today I saw Ellen for the last time. I shall miss her more than I can ever say. She was out by the old tree. She was laughing and standing on the branch the swing was tied onto, the way she always did. She called to me to get on the swing and I did and she hooked her feet around the ropes and helped push me. We'd done it a thousand times. I laughed and swung and look up at her until I was dizzy. She climbed higher, looking down at me and called, "You can do it on your own now. Go as high as you want to."

Memories...you have them...I know you have. Like driving down the street or walking along and suddenly, there's a huge old tree with branches extending in all directions from a solid, hearty trunk and it catches your attention. The thought comes, "Wouldn't that be fun to climb, or put a swing in, or picnic under, or just plain sit under on a warm day."

Ellen had a tree like that on her farm. They had a wind break of trees along the wheat field. It was large break of trees, almost a small forest. The cows used to like to get in there on warm days. There were a lot of grassy areas. The old tree stood in the middle of this grassy area. It had a really big gnarled bump on the side where lightning had cleaved off a huge branch one summer. Ellen and I could almost touch fingers when we stood on either side of the tree and stretched our arms out just as far as we could reach. Her Gramps had put the swing on it and her dad put up a new one every spring. He said to keep it safe for us monkeys, but we caught him in it once in awhile.

Our two families had lots of picnics out there in the summer and Ellen and I ate our lunch out there sometimes. After we finished chores my mom or Ellen's would pack us some sandwiches and something to drink and we'd spend the rest of the afternoon climbing and swinging and just laying on our backs watching the clouds move over the top of the branches. Ellen was game for anything. She couldn't wait to try something new or exciting or just plain different. She led...I followed and she led a merry chase.

And if you want to slip away into a fairyland this was surely the place to come in the winter just after a fresh snowfall or one of those days when an ice storm had just gone through. We always managed to get away for awhile on those days, sometimes Dad came, too. He said it was hard to believe something as destructive as those storms could create something so incredibly beautiful as that windbreak covered in fresh snow or clear sparkling ice. He took a couple of photos with it looking that way, and I still have them. Magic!

I also have a picture of Ellen on the swing, taken earlier that fall. She's laughing; her feet are way up, almost touching the golden leaves and her hair is flying out behind her. The tree stands out clearly, its gold-filled branches reaching wide, leaves blowing slightly in the breeze, her hair, almost the same color.

Ellen liked to play jokes. Her very favorite was to hide and then jump out yelling, "BOO!" and scare you. She did it to everyone she knew. She got in trouble at school more than once for doing it. She loved hiding...sometimes she scared you and sometimes she called out to you to find her. And she loved that tree, more than anyone, she loved that old tree. So did I.

Her farm is gone now. Her parents sold it and the people who bought it built houses on the land. My folks bought the windbreak. It touched our land and Dad was afraid the developers would cut down the trees and he felt it was a good idea to keep them there. I think he bought it as sort of an apology to Ellen.

That last Labor Day weekend, my family was going to the State Fair at the fairgrounds in Springfield, and as a treat they said Ellen could come with us. We were really looking forward to it. The rides, the games, the food and the animal judging; we could hardly wait.

But then Ellen had to play that stupid game again. She went and hid in the barn and I couldn't find her. When Mom went out and called to tell her we were leaving she jumped out and scared Mom so bad she dropped the fruit salad she was carrying and broke the bowl. Mom was so mad she sent Ellen home and said she couldn't go with us. Even though I cried they didn't relent, because they said she had to learn scaring people wasn't funny. I didn't have as much fun without her.

When we got home Ellen was dead. Her father's bull had gotten loose and she was trampled.

Her mom had packed her a picnic lunch and she'd gone out to the tree. While she was there the bull broke loose and went into the grassy place and found her there and chased her. She ran to the tree to climb out of the way, but it failed her...the branch she grabbed was old and dry and it broke. The bull was found later...grazing peacefully, still in the grassy place. Her dad went crazy and killed the bull and cut down the tree and tried to burn the stump out. Right after that, they sold the farm – they said they couldn't stand to live here anymore. That's when Dad bought the windbreak.

I went out there after the funeral, feeling so alone. I sat on the grass by the burned stump and cried. I felt it was all my fault because I had not found her in the barn that day, before Mom did. While I was crying I felt a hand on my shoulder and heard Ellen's voice talking to me. She said it wasn't my fault – to stop crying.

The next spring a small shoot was growing out of the stump. It has continued to grow and over the years I've talked with Ellen now and again. She has always been there for me when I needed her.

And today, my very special day, my wedding day, I came out early to share with Ellen. She was laughing and standing on the branch the swing was tied onto...she climbed higher and she called, "You can do it on your own, now. Go as high as you want to." and then she was gone. I know she's right, but I shall miss her more than I can ever say.

Flying Over Iowa
(The Power of the Imagination) by Kathleen Bogan

You want to detach,
suspend yourself in soft dark space.
Inhale the blue. Below
white clouds begin to huddle,
dream of warmth before
advancing night.

You recognize how roads
drive the pattern of the fields;
watch trailer trucks slip down
slick green highways. They are bullets
in slow motion
in the barrel of a gun.

Then something, specks
of things, float up
from the unfamiliar earth;
bewildered cows tumbling
in the jetstream, hogs, hounds,
a tabby cat. Two
just-washed children, faces
pressed to your porthole,
captured, astonished to be
no longer gazing out
their kitchen window, but in,
at the you they imagined as you
passed over, imagining them.

An Antidote to Football Saturdays

by Meredith Campbell

They hadn't made the labyrinth on purpose to escape foot-ball mania, but it had served them well. Every home game Satur-day morning, Julia and Laura gently kissed their sleeping hus-bands and children good-bye, then raced for their vans. Out in the country, on some property Julia's aunt had left her, they'd pains-takingly built the labyrinth path by path, stone by stone, modeling it on the labyrinth of the minotaur in ancient Crete. Near the dirt road next to it, they met at 8 o'clock sharp, Julia climbing into Laura's van with a thermos of coffee.

"Getting out here this early is going to kill me one of these times," Julia gasped and slammed the door shut. "I need coffee now!" Laura silently held out two mugs and Julia poured.

"Ahhhh!" Laura sighed and leaned back, her face wreathed in steam from the mug. "But have you considered the alternative?"

"Oh, yeah, I remember it well. Streams of people dressed in red everywhere I go, and the damned pregame, game, and post-game blaring into every store."

"That hush during the plays, the zombie look on everyone's face as they listen!"

Julia snorted. "All those out-of-town drivers going the wrong way on one-way streets with their horns honking, hanging out the windows of their cars hollering, 'Go, Big Red!'"

"So, rushing out here before all that starts isn't really such a sacrifice, is that what you're saying now that you've had your cof-fee?"

"Something like that. Ready?"

Laura reached in the back seat and grabbed her purple carry-all. "Ready. I'll surprise you with what I gathered for our lunch?"

"Absolutely."

They jumped out of the van and made their way through the tall grasses, past the stream, to the sandy spot where they'd made their labyrinth. They stopped for a moment just outside the opening, scanning the curving paths neatly marked by stones placed at intervals.

"God, what a maze!" Julia marvelled, then burst out laughing. "It just a-mazes me."

Laura shook her head. "How hard it must be for you – being quite crazy."

"Yeah. Sometimes it is."

She drew a deep breath. "Let's go!"

"In here to the left, and we start around." They set out among the stones until they found themselves turning and walking on a path next to the one they'd been on before. "A tortuous route to the center," Laura exclaimed as they doubled back the way they'd just been, but on a different path.

"We twist and turn in an ancient labyrinth, inside a cave. It's cold and dark and we've lost our way," moaned Julia dramatically. "We're imprisoned here and unless we can get to the center and find our way back out, we could wander forever, until we turn into skeletons. Years from now, they'll find our bones!"

"I can feel the walls closing in. The passage is growing narrow now. Feel the spider webs; it's a long, long time since anyone has passed this way," Laura's horror-filled voice drifted back to Julia.

"It really does feel different this time," Julia whispered. "Eerie."

"I know. That wailing wind." She shivered. "But we've got to press on. Our lives depend on it." Just before the center, she paused and motioned to Julia to squeeze next to her. Together, in total quiet, they opened their canteens and solemnly spilled a few drops of water onto the exact middle of the circle. Hastily replacing the tops, they clasped hands and stepped into the center of the labyrinth.

Instantly there was a swooshing sound and they felt themselves whirling, spinning, deep, ever deeper toward the vortex of a spiral enclosing them. Laura lost her hold on Julia's hand, so violent was the twisting agitation that gripped them. They turned and tumbled until – how long it was they forgot to think – they landed on their backsides with a small jolt.

Laura heard a loud growl, followed by muffled roars. "Julia, is that you?" she asked hesitantly into the darkness.

Suddenly a bright beacon of light lit up the cavern and Laura cried out. "Just me," Julia's voice echoed. "Knocked myself in the face in the dark getting out my flashlight, then I couldn't turn it on at first. Made me mad!"

"Right. I thought for a moment...Well, I thought maybe we'd found the minotaur."

"Ha ha. But we *are* back in our cave in ancient Crete." Julia's flashlight swept the ceiling of delicate stalactites, then trained on a dramatic stalagmite formation in the center. "Our beautiful long-haired stalagmite woman!"

Laura stood and moved toward it, circled it, gently gliding her palm along its white surface. "Luminous – like it's lit from within," she marveled.

Suddenly she froze. "Julia. Music. People are coming."

"Oh m'God. Up through the path we always leave by. What'll we do?"

" Hide. No telling what might happen if they find us here. Quick, squeeze into that niche, back as far as you can get. The music's getting louder."

Inside, Julia switched off her flashlight and they huddled to-gether. "Just in time," Julia hissed, as the cave lit up and two women in long blue dresses stepped inside holding fiery torches of burn-ing rushes. They held them high on either side of the opening to the labyrinth as one by one, a procession of musicians came through into the center. Finally, two lamp bearers in golden gowns appeared, carrying stone lamps from which rose flame and thin columns of smoke.

The four fire-bearers moved to equidistant points along the walls of the cave, transforming it into a richly illuminated stone sanctuary of long shadows and mystery. The musicians began cir-cling the stalagmite woman in an intricate dance.

One woman blew on double pipes, touching the fingers of both hands deftly to the holes in the slender, flute-like instruments. Merrily, she tossed her long, dark curls in time to the notes' rapid rhythm. Another clashed cymbals, clasped high over her head. Next to her, the triton shell player blew through a hole in her huge seashell for a trumpeting sound. Alternate dancers moving in opposite directions, they wove among each other in a snaky spiral.

Two women shook sistrums, each holding hers high by one corner with her left hand, touching the rungs of the ladder-like instrument with her right. They smiled at each other as first one, then the other sistrum jingled. Then came two lyre players, sweeping the seven strings of their tortoise-shell soundboards with the points of triangular ivory blades.

Without warning, Julia wriggled forward and started moving toward the dancers. Laura half rose, lunged and grabbed her round the middle with both arms before she could reach them. Hauling her backwards, Laura staggered, but managed to pull Julia back into the niche.

"What fresh hell is this?" Laura hissed in Julia's ear, still hanging onto her for fear she'd leap out again. Julia shook her head and blinked.

"I don't know. I felt like I was in a trance and had to follow them." She gave a last, vigorous shake of her head and murmured wistfully, "I don't know what would have been so bad about it."

"Well, I suppose if you didn't knock into them or anything, stayed away from the torches, were invisible in Crete like usual, and came out of your trance in time to not abandon me here – to say nothing of your family – everything would have been ducky!" Laura said between gritted teeth.

Julia turned to watch the dancers again. "Thanks, Laura," she finally whispered. Around and around they circled, a blur of blues, yellows and greens, the dancers now twirling with coils of hair spiralling outward like long black snakes. The music was high-pitched and sweet, growing faster and louder until it suddenly ceased.

One by one, each player set a shiny object in a crevice in the tall stalagmite woman, most in her long, flowing hair. They stepped back then and the fire-bearers advanced to place their treasures.

The torch bearers moved slowly out into the labyrinth, and that was the signal for the music to begin again, accompanied this time by singing. The procession continued, until only the lamp-bearers remained, and soon they too had filed out. For a moment, Laura and Julia could still hear the music clearly, but soon it grew faint, louder once more – then died away.

"Whew!" Laura pushed out of the niche, threw down her carry-all and sank against a wall. Julia flicked on her flashlight and surveyed the stalagmite woman with admiration. "Just look at her now – absolutely glittering with decorations – even jewels."

"That was some ceremony you almost joined. What would I have told Jim and Leslie and Louise about your abandoning them here – 3500 years ago in ancient Crete?"

Julia began to laugh. "The truth, I guess. That I'd become a priestess to the goddess. They'd understand, don't you think?"

"Oh, yeah. Absolutely, So, where do you want to explore before we twirl back home through that labyrinth we made outside of Knossos?"

"We've got a few hours until the football game's over. I though we could wander through the market, maybe find some of those snake-goddess figurines."

Laura stood up, brushed herself off, and looked around. "Okay. Let's go. The priestesses should all be out of the labyrinth by now. By the way, how do you plan to explain the snake-goddess figurines to your family?"

Julia smiled. "The truth, again. I'll just say I spent the day shopping in Crete. And they'll assume I mean Crete, Nebraska."

Suitcase of Language:
A Woman Writer in Chicago by Cheryl Chaffin

*"Language is where you live, it's a real place,
more important than geography."*
— Jonathan Raban

An entry in her notebook dated April 14 reads, "How can I not be happy?" and outlines her future plans of full-time writing while living with her lover in Chicago. But on May 18 her words say she wants a place to call her own. Rather than coming to Chicago to live with John, she opts for housesitting in Taos, New Mexico, and places an ad the following day in the *Taos News.*

"Incredible housekeeper seeks incredible house, graduate student, writer," states the ad. She gives her first name and phone number on the second line, and on May 31 gets a response from two women in New York City who have left their three-bedroom house 30 miles north of Taos due to a serious car accident and one woman's need for physical therapy. They require a caretaker for seven cats and two dogs. The animals must stay in the house since coyotes, likely to dine on felines and fight with dogs, roam the dry plains above the Rio Grande.

John is visiting her in California when she receives the women's message. He is surprised at her decision to live in Taos, but supportive. He wonders aloud when and if she will come to

Chicago and when he'll see her again. They agreed that with her acceptance to Goddard College, into a low residency Masters program in creative writing, she would live rent-free in his quiet garden apartment where she could spend days reading and writing and have access to the myriad libraries, literary events and writers to be found in the country's third largest metropolis.

Yet, the high desert of New Mexico has always felt like a second, surrogate home to her, as it has for numerous others. For a long time, she'd read predominantly authors living in the Southwest - Native Americans, Chicanos, women who had either lived in the region or had been magnetized to it as she had.

Today she sits at an antique desk, carved for a left-handed teacher and probably used in a one-room Illinois schoolhouse. On the desk there is a computer, a stack of papers containing her writing, some reference books, photos in frames, a card that cites ways to be an artist. She reads the card periodically while sitting at the desk, in what is now both her and John's apartment. The card says, "Stay loose. Make friends with freedom and uncertainty. Cultivate moods. Have wild imaginings, transformative dreams and perfect calm." It also suggests having someone dangerous to tea, taking naps, building a fort and swinging high into the moonlight on a swingset.

Yesterday she swung with John on the swings at Oz Park. It was early evening, after dinner at a Greek restaurant, and fog shrouded the tip of the Sears Tower. Their feet seemed to touch the purple night sky as a small boy watched them.

"Do you want to swing?" she asked him. An empty swing hung limp beside her. "We're big kids. We love to swing." He smiled and hurried up the steps of a nearby ladder, his curly, dark head disappearing into a maze of slides, tunnels and bars.

They also took a nap. She slept and intermittently read a book written by a woman living alone on a Maine island for several months.

Would she have done these things in New Mexico? She may have built a fort at the edge of the desert, its walls a padding of dry, dense sagebrush. She could have invited someone danger-ous - a Harley Davidson rider or a desert wanderer? - to tea?

Whether or not she is in the high desert of New Mexico or the Midwest metropolis of Chicago, she's caught in the net of creating. She has not given up her dream to live in Taos; but she dwells here, now. Her stories are not those of the desert but are formed in a flat, linear spread of city that stretches to the shore of a great lake. But they are her stories regardless. She is writing and dreaming. In this place her stories come to dwell.

But this place holds painful memories, not for her but for her mother who was married for 24 years and has been divorced for ten, and is angry at her daughter as she prepares for a move to Chicago.
"You're not trying hard enough. You're giving up your own desires, losing self-definition by living with a man in a city you'd never choose to live in on your own," she accuses her.

Not only is her daughter sacrificing freedom of choice and mobility for a man, just as she had done herself, but is leaving for Chicago, the same city that she herself had moved to 30 years ago and returned from four years later.

* * *

In 1965 a young mother and her new husband of two years had packed their belongings into a shimmering blue convertible Thunderbird, put their toddler into the backseat with her toys, books and blanket and left California headed for Cary, Illinois, then a tiny suburb 45 miles north and west of Chicago. The mother, who had grown up in California and developed a passion for travel as a child while visiting relatives in Iowa by train with her mother, thought this move would be an adventure, a new and exciting destination.

And it was an adventure; of harsh winters in an isolated town raising two children (a baby was born in Chicago within two years of the move) , driving a convertible without snow tires on slick winter roads. Her husband, a salesman, traveled for three and four weeks at a stretch. The baby had jaundice and the little girl had too much energy, wanting constantly to go out and play in the snow and in the summers trying to run outside at the approaching greenish-gray air of tornado winds that blew the prairie grasses flat, pasting them to the ground. The woman made curtains for all the rooms in their new house and sewed school dresses for her daughter about to enter kindergarden. She baked pies and cookies and cakes, and gained weight. She got a job as a receptionist at the McHenry County Hospital, then quit in two weeks due to morning sickness. Her father fell 20 feet from a ladder while painting a house in California. On the four hour flight from Chicago to Los Angeles she sobbed uncontrollably, and by the time she reached the hospital he had died from internal injuries.

She assured her mother that Chicago would not be the same place for her as it had been for the older woman. To her mother Chicago had meant bondage to a house and two children, the painful reminder of loneliness and a dead father. For the daughter Chicago symbolized creative space and freedom.

* * *

Here her schedule is her own. She wakes when she wants to, makes coffee and reads, writes for an hour or two. She stretches, goes for walks, writes letters, poems and stories. She teaches classes in English as a Second Language near Logan Square. The apartment is still and quiet. The air is light with rain trickling and tapping down the drainpipe just outside the kitchen door. Cicadas rattle their heat-inspired crescendos. She revises a poem she will read at a poetry performance tonight. Books are her only children, crowding the shelves across from her writing desk, and she does not make cookies and cakes to nurture herself or her family. She makes stories and poems.

She wants her mother, now attending the university and applying to graduate school, to trust that her daughter can live her desires. She wants her to know her daughter's strength. Must she live for her mother the life she did not have, failed to claim because she was afraid her dreams were the wrong ones? Might her mother have known different dreams had she been born in another time or place? She has in the past been the answer to the life her mother missed, a life not available to the good girl who grew up in a minister's household in the 1950s.

Only recently has she begun the creation of a life lived truly for herself, alone in the house since her two children have moved out. And the daughter, in turn, discovers that these days are her own, remembering Annie Dillard's words, "How you spend your days is how you spend your life."

She will mold her days carefully, consciously, shaped from her own questions while 2,000 miles away her mother shapes her days. Perhaps, as Rilke said, together and apart they will live themselves one distant day into the answers.

The Men of Nebraska by Marilyn Coffey

Straight-legged and tight-lipped they walk
the men on the main streets of Lincoln

Faces crease as neatly as perma-press seams
ironed by a life pursuing the rectangular

A life run as straight as their streets, as narrow:
laid out at right angles to the known earth's four corners.

Behind their eyes: ticker tapes repeat various prices
of cattle (up) and hogs (down) at yesterday's markets.

Behind their eyes spin constant weather reports:
inches of rainfall calculated to the second decimal.

Behind their eyes sweeps a tornado of the immeasurable:
Of curves not straightened. Of whirls and eddies. Of tides.

Down the streets of Nebraska stiff shadows approach.
They size me up. A lid flickers. It's a small problem

for men used to assessing the value of a brood mare,
or pricing a thresher. Their eyes barely ripple my bodice.

Is she used? Do the breasts function? their eyes narrow.
Hey, baby, has anybody oiled that cunt lately?

My heart crashes to the flat pavement. A false alarm.
The tight-lidded men of Nebraska walk stiff-leggedly on.

Winter Sweets by Marilyn Coffey

Snow lies like thick frosting
on earth's frozen cake

Eastward, sun's hot tongue
licks red the smooth rim

Like dark toys, two horses
prance in an outdated corral

Nostril breath whirls white
as modern auto exhaust
trembles above the highway

Overhead, wind stirs neither
tree tips nor phone wires.

The Sexual Auction
by Lyn Coffin

Emil liked the way they'd presented the item - the room, the decorations - but was disconcerted by the appearance of the item herself. He'd expected someone younger, he said.

His uncle teased him. "I keep forgetting you're not from the Midwest," he said. "I probably should have taken you to the virgin auction first. Perhaps I hoped you would take to this superior form of the spectacle as I did at your age. Skipping stages is a trait of the males in our family, but you're your mother's child, so I might have known."

By the time Emil recovered from his uncle's jibes, the item had been positioned. He'd expected the item's hands and legs to be tied. But Emil, gifted with the capacity for quick internalization, had no sooner told himself he was disappointed, than he questioned and corrected himself, and discovered the opposite was actually true. His hope in thinking along the lines of fetters or bonds was to have the item's subservience emphasized. But the lack of bonds did the job more effectively.

The item's physical configuration was being discussed by his uncle and several others. Their remarks seemed to Emil in poor taste. He decided to listen and let himself be instructed. When his uncle asked his opinion, Emil was reluctant. He responded in a low voice, worthy of his mother's delicate murmurings, but his uncle showed no corresponding delicacy – indeed, he demanded Emil speak up like a man. Emil had no choice but to obey.

"Well, uncle, leaving aside considerations of age, I find the item almost perfect in every respect save one: she appears, to my untutored eye at least, somewhat on the pear-shaped side of things."

His uncle surely was able to hear Emil without straining, yet he kept his right hand cupped behind his ear even after the young man had finished his appraisal. The gesture gave him a particularly gleeful and idiotic appearance. Emil regretfully decided against describing the gesture in his next letter. Surely, his mother would not take kindly to having her brother made fun of by her son.

"Pear-shaped, boy?" his uncle responded. "Pear-shaped? You find the corn-fed little lady pear-shaped, do you?"

His uncle's reiteration irritated Emil. When he'd been eight and his sister six, she teased him by repeating words. "I want to go to town," Emil would say. "You want to go to town?" his sister would echo, her little mocking mouth gleaming with baby teeth. "To town?" she would repeat, as if incredulous, and this had seemed to Emil the cruelest form of mockery.

Emil was surprised to find his chin grasped in his uncle's hand. His uncle directed his attention back to the item, continuing: "Pear-shaped she is, my boy. Of course, the pear-shaped item has long been cherished here as the ideal of feminine beauty. Perhaps it is true, as many today believe, that one's aesthetic is a reflection of one's geography. Perhaps we, in our midway country, have developed an aesthetic ideal midway between the large-breasted, hourglass ideal of your father's people to the North, and the vegetable-stalk formation cherished and fiercely defended by the barbarians of the South."

Emil wished his uncle would stop talking. He was busy taking the item in with all the eye for detail a young man is apt to have. She was about thirty, perhaps even older, but beautifully kept up. Her skin was white and dewy as a girl's, and her stomach so flat one could clearly discern the outlines of both hip-bones. Emil admired the way they had posed her on the apricot velvet drape, and was delighted by the slow rotation of the bed, affording all an equally delicious view.

He was especially fascinated by the styling of the item's long, dark hair, which cascaded over the globes of her breasts, down the slope of her ribcage and across the plain of her stomach in long, wavering strands like a curtain of black lace, the ends of the strands curling into the slightly lighter tuft of lower hair, where each was secured with a tiny ribbon. But just as Emil had decided her front was the item's best aspect, they eased her onto her left side and had her kneel on the bed, chest to knees.

From where Emil sat, it was possible to see only these things: her small heels, the bent, pink toes and tissue-y white soles of her feet, and the smooth dome of her ass, looking as firm and almost-hard as a new apple. The smallness of the item's toes, peeking out from under that great white dome, touched Emil to the quick. Each of her firm white cheeks was underscored by a scimitar curve of thigh, and it struck him that the jolly cartoon faces he had once drawn on the backs of schoolbooks were, seen in retrospect, nothing less than primitive attempts to anticipate that globe, those cheeks, those curves.

His uncle made a noise - half chuckle, half moan, the kind of noise in which only a middle-aged, overweight man would indulge. For the first time, Emil smiled - the half-heedless, half-reflective smile of a handsome young man.

By this time, the item had revolved a half turn. She lay now on her right side. Her small feet were all that was clearly visible to Emil. For some reason, this innocent, lengthwise view of the item excited him more than the others. Forgetting his uncle's instructions, Emil leaned forward, wanting to touch, to land one fingertip somewhere on the sole of one perfect foot.

But the bed had been placed at just that distance from the immovable seats that no one, however long his arms, could touch the item. The item continued to revolve slowly, tantalizingly, just out of reach. Now Emil understood the need for the seatbelts and the unfastening penalties.

With a great effort of will, Emil managed to sit back, feeling his sex stir outrageously. Fearing the ridicule of his uncle and his uncle's friends, Emil tented his newspaper over his lap so any further activity there would be under cover of newsprint.

When Emil returned to full-scale observation, he found himself staring into the item's nipples. The soft pink circles reminded him of the eyes of the one stuffed animal his parents had permitted him. The white plush elephant had black button eyes, backed with pink felt. After a while, the buttons came off. Emil's mother volunteered to replace them, but Emil said he preferred the elephant without buttons - completely soft, perfectly embraceable.

No sooner had Emil come out of this reverie than the item lowered herself onto the pillow. Now her breasts were twin prows pushing through an apricot satin sea, and it was into her eyes Emil found himself staring. They were blue, clear, each with its long black fringe of lash. They seemed to promise nothing, to permit everything. And now Emil remembered: his sister's doll had such eyes and it was because of her complaints about Emil's always taking her doll that his parents had allowed him the elephant. In time, the blue-glass eyes of the doll had come to seem hostile and Emil had ceased coveting her.

As it turned out, the item's eyes resulted in her being given an eight-and-under rating. Emil heard several older men protesting the arbitrariness of this decision – "So much attention paid to eyes - Unheard of!" Emil turned to his uncle. "How can those old fools give her two demerits for round eyes when -"

His uncle smiled, put a finger to his lips and whispered, "They're my friends, son. And this may be your lucky day."

The reason for his mysterious comment was revealed when, after a few minutes, the chief judge announced that Item Number 63 had been sold to none other than Emil's uncle.

They led her over. The young man's embarrassment overtook excitement for the moment. As Emil leapt to his feet, his member abruptly subsided, allowing the newspaper he had held in his lap an uninterrupted slide to the floor.

"She's for you, boy," Emil's uncle said proudly, thrusting the item in Emil's direction. "It was the lower rating, you see. Never could have afforded her otherwise."

Confused, Emil found himself staring down past one pink, perfect nipple at the front page of the fallen paper.

"Thank you, uncle," Emil managed to say.

"You're welcome, lad. I don't know how you'll get her home, or explain her to your mother, but I'm sure you'll think of something!"

Emil looked at his pink-cheeked uncle. "I don't know," he announced. "I just know what I'll do with her as soon as I get the chance!"

Even the judges cheered at this, and Emil's uncle beamed. The young man didn't have the heart to show his uncle the headline he had just glimpsed: "War Feared With North/ Border Closed."

Besides, when he again looked down, that headline had been erased, completely covered as it was by one pink, perfect foot.

Michigan Pigs on Pilgrimage by Lyn Coffin

The pilgrim pigs of Arenac are coming,
Rolling south on Interstate 75.
Sows and boars thrum to visions of Miami –
Pinker than roses they are, rounder-eyed
Then children – rosy magnitude of flesh, they
Come! They roll through Au Gres, salmon capital
of Michigan, then Omer, where the Rifle
River bends, Standish with its mousy houses,
Pinconning with small churches, big yellow wheels
Of cheese... Rolling down the asphalt, their pristine
Flesh declares itself in parables, glows
Like rubies, like rosy erasers in
The gray hands of a school-teacherly dawn.
Their doxology swells: "We are the clean ones,
Baptized beside the Singing Bridge! Saginaw
Bay cannot distract us, we are anointed
By the sun!" South they roll, each hoof held steady
On stainless steel casters and mother of pearl.

Deep in Chicago, Deep in the Night

by Carol Cowen

Sally stayed away from Chicago for as long as she could, before returning to Lakeshore Drive and the frozen blocks of brown grass that stretched like bristly doormats along a gray choppy lake. She chose winter to come back, so that she could dislike the city the most, and remember best the reasons she had left it for California so many years before.

She returned to the apartment of her childhood, not the actual apartment, but one similar to the ones that nestled her as she grew up, first on the far south side and later on the near north, as her family became more affluent.

The apartment has dark wood floors, gouged and scarred from decades of tricycles propelled by small children, floors now polished and varnished to a sheen capable of showing off the Turkish and Native American rugs of her hosts - her daughter Laura and her girlfriend Celeste. The same wood floors extend into the kitchen, where smaller versions of the rugs soak up the drops of water Sally leaves after doing the dishes at the old white porcelain sink.

Laura and Celeste are curled up on the futon/sofa when Sally enters the living room.

"Thanks, Mom," Laura says, smiling.

"Yeah, Mom, thanks!" Celeste grins at her, watching Sally's stance to see if it changes as she calls her "Mom." Sally only plops down in an armchair and picks up the copy of Bay Times that she has brought with her from San Francisco.

"What are you reading, Mom?" Laura asks, sitting up from the blanket where she is snuggled with Celeste.

"Well, if you must know, the personals. I figure if you can be so happy with a girlfriend, maybe I should try one, too." Sally addresses her words directly at Celeste, challenging her, but Celeste is asleep and only snores softly.

"Oh, Mom, you're as hetero as they come. What would Dad say?"

"I try not to think about him," Sally says, her voice lowering and scratchy like an old record. The room is silent except for the hiss of the radiators, toasting the three in late night heat. Sally looks back at her paper, but after awhile she gazes at the three living room windows, lined up in a row in exactly the same spot as they were in her grandparents' apartment of fifty years ago. As a small child she had gazed out of such windows, sitting in a wicker rocker, rocking in the warm night breeze as gauze curtains fluttered in and out of the dusty screens and windowsills. The Northwestern trains rolled along on tracks only a block away, perpetually stirring dust in the open-windowed apartment.

To see the same views now, after living in so many other apartments and houses in two countries and six states, feels strange, as if she's not really been anywhere.

"What are you thinking, Mom?" Laura asks, slipping quietly out of the futon, where Celeste is sleeping. She sits on the rug at Sally's feet, and puts her chin on Sally's knee. Sally laughs and runs her fingers through Laura's hair.

This apartment – it's so much like my grandparents', like apartments I grew up in. It even smells the same, a combination of coffee, soap, radiator heat and old apartment walls, layered in too many coats of paint. The walls of my grandparents' apartment got painted every seven years. I remember the flurry of work beforehand, piling all the furniture in the middle of the room and covering it all with sheets before the painters came, They painted the walls white, always white . . ."

"Were you happy then?"

Sally thinks about this. "I was, even though I didn't have a mother. I had all those grandparents and aunts to spoil me. Visiting here has helped me remember how much I liked it. It's like a gift you've given me." Sally looks at her oldest daughter, her hand now still, tears gathering in her eyes.

"Oh, Mom. You miss him, don't you. Dad, I mean."

"I hate him. I hate him and I miss him. And I **hate** the nights."

"I thought you'd be out doing the bar scene, having some fun, finally."

"I'm afraid I'll run into him."

"In San Francisco? Oh, please." Laura gets up, looking disgusted, and shakes herself. Sally thinks she looks like an Irish setter in socks. Laura nudges Celeste and pulls her hand out from the blanket.

"C'mon, girl, it's time for bed." Celeste wakes up, smiles and starts to say something before she remembers Laura's mother is still in the room. Instead she says, "Goodnight, Mrs. Crandall. See you in the morning."

"You can forget the 'Mrs.,' Sally says. "Sally will do. Goodnight, you two. I'll just stay up a bit and take in the view."

Sally moves to the end of the futon and stares out the window into the courtyard of the apartment complex, its three yellow brick buildings formed in a U, just like her grandparents' building. It is after midnight, but in three apartments there are small squares of color blazing, three televisions still glowing deep into the night. Somehow these three spots of color seem more lonely than if all of the trio-ed sets of windows were dark, as they were when she was a girl. People talked to each other then or made love or slept, but now they sit, drawn to the television as insects are to light. She wonders if she will be like them, one of these single people for the rest of her life.

The sizzling radiator turns off with a clunk, and the room is silent. Outside the car sounds are muffled, sucked up by the thick, wet flakes of snow that have begun to fall. She looks out the window again, and sees the three spots of color change to two, one extinguished with a quick click. Was the clicker an old person, long since asleep in her chair and just now waking to get up and go to bed? Or an insomniac who finally caught a glimpse of the sandman?

She smiles at herself for this childish reference. She remembers believing there really was an old man with a sack who visited all of the apartments, one after the other, sprinkling the sand that sparkled like gold dust. She would lay awake in her grandmother's bed, listening to the commuter train whistles and waiting each night for her magic sprinkles.

Now she lies back on the futon, drowsy in the dry air, mesmerized by the falling flakes illuminated by the courtyard lamps. She hears footsteps padding through the thickening snow, moving up the courtyard walk towards their building. She falls asleep before she knows whether or not the steps are the sandman's.

The Wait by Jo Lee Dibert-Fitko

Last year's
cornfield
pokes through
the snow.
Barn wood whimpers
as woods sting
their home.
Spiney trees naked
from greenery's
desertion
stretch angular limbs.
Snap from your stare.
Molded trails,
rusting tractors,
halt at frozen fences
while dirt mounds
protrude like
mosaic kitchen tiles.
Puffed up skies weep
grey-tinged flakes
on winter's livestock
huddled.
Muted lyrics,
stored in silos and
the hollows of space
count the days,
release their voice
in this season of wait
to the first green blade
of spring.

To Pass the Time by Sharon Dornberg-Lee

first hot day of the year   you and I
sit down out back in the garden   to play a little
gin rummy
                    pass the time
you shuffle the deck   Kool hanging from your lips
            long brown fingers work from memory
memory stored in the hands   sends the cards
arcing   intermixing   snapping under your touch

but you deal my first card face UP and play
                    this is the way they play...
a way I've never seen:
                    ...on the south side
jokers and twos wild   spreads thrown down
discard pile fanned open
                    you take what you need
you can even play off my cards
                    's called hitchin'
you get points for what you've played
                    so play high
                    that's the strategy of the game

but my way:
you keep your cards close to your chest   you wait
til you've won and shout out
                                    "Gin!" and slam
down all your cards at once
                    *and that's gin rummy? you call **that** gin rummy?*
but still when it's my turn you say
                    it's three of diamonds to you   just like my dad

I get both jokers in the first hand and win
                    my way   nothing's wild

51

The Scientific Property of Self Organized Criticality

by Kelly Easton

It is an old story. He is hung over again. She is sour. He stares at the newspaper, not seeing the words. The letters are scurrying ticks across the page. He smashes the ticks but no blood comes. She stands with a coffee mug watching the news. She is calling to someone, calling them baby. He lifts up his head. Could she be calling him? But no, she is speaking to the television set, and when she sees his face, it's like the whole of human history explodes in her skull. "I want you out of here by noon." She turns. The coffee in her mug sloshes over the slogan on her mug, When Life Gives You Lemons – Hide.

"I have had enough," she continues, so he just drifts to some cold clean place, some Switzerland where she's reduced to an old silent movie in front of him. She is a skier racing out of control, down down down the alpine slope, but then he slips up and listens:

"Someone's got to do something"; she grabs her absurd pink purse, big enough to hold the state of Texas, weird enough to belong to Mary Poppins. "I am going to save those babies."

And he thinks, there are babies somewhere she is going to save them and it could be anywhere she is going. And she is gone. Panic, then relief as he realizes that CNN will repeat on the half hour. He will find out about the babies then and he can save them too, save her, save himself, but first a drink to steady his nerves.

She searches for the keys to her car. They are down there somewhere, in the deep sea that is her purse, and damn, if she doesn't find them she will never help the babies, because it was there on the national news, in her very own town, about the suffering babies and the urgent need for people to volunteer; time, money, or both. She has one of the two, but if she doesn't find the keys, if she returns to the house, to its stench of beer, the flood of pee still on the closet floor, then she will not get out again, not this time, not ever. She sweeps the purse with her hand. The keys come out like a grab bag gift which is a sign, she thinks, of miracles to come.

He looks for a beer, a drop, anything, but she has poured out every drop, including the bottle of cognac Sylvester Stallone had given their son for his work on a movie. And she has taken his car keys, his wallet, everything; let him suffer. To hell with him. She starts the engine of the Buick. To hell with her. He licks the remaining drop out of a bottle of scotch retrieved from a nose dive in the sink. To hell with her superiority.

The Buick carries her down familiar streets. Just right, she had told him in younger days. Just right, this small Midwestern city, its contrast of plains and jutting buildings. Just right. There is a children's story she knows like this but she just can't catch it. She will tell it to the babies as she holds them in her arms. She will not tell them the scary ones, the ones more true to life and the trees are white lashes against the winter air.

In the downtown, there was a parade. The streets are littered with streamers. Children climb on the empty bleachers, their scarves dangling from their necks. A blind man walks with a woman in pink, who guides him around a downed tree, over a step to the pedestrian walk, and it occurs to her now that it is the woman who is blind, not the man. The blind leading the blind.

She reads the address as she rolls through a stop and calls to a boy if he knows the way. The boy points vaguely. She parks, but his directions don't work, and her husband is calling, but not to her. He is calling down an enamel well. He thinks he's lost something, that there's more in there than just his insides and she fumbles in her pocket, wishes she hadn't stopped smoking. The air is brisk, brisk enough to kill the elderly. Every year, there are an unlucky few whose electricity is shut off, who die of the cold. If she laid down here, went to sleep on the street, she may wake up dead. She laughs at her own joke, hah hah, wake up...dead.

He brushes his teeth, an attempt at civility. He swallows the Listerine, then finishes the bottle. She walks past a shop, past the steps of a church, through busy holiday bodies, to a less inhabited part of town and then she finds it; a white brick number on an empty street. The building stretches forward. It opens. It opens. A Christmas tree winks through the clinic glass doors. Come.

She sighs with relief and enters, ready to tell her story, ready to be embraced and then taken to the babies. She will hold them in her arms, stay all night, or even live there.

We have a waiting list for these positions, the woman at the desk tells her, shoving a form and a medical history at her. But I mean to *volunteer*. The woman attempts a smile; donations are always wanted, more necessary than love, she thinks she hears the woman add, maybe not.

She fills out the lengthy form.

He takes a shower, as lousy as he feels, in preparation for her return. He splashes on cologne to diffuse the Listerine smell. She will open the door. Maybe she'll drop her keys, she often does. He will pick them up for her, say, Sorry Baby. And she will forgive him. Again.

Now she listens to the woman at the desk who tells her that the news story was filmed a year ago, when they first opened. People have come forward, the woman says, the world is not so cynical after all, or so scared. People will hold the babies, she says, it's the most popular volunteer gig in town. People will hold the babies with AIDS.

She writes them a check, the last forty dollars in her account, and doesn't bother to tell the woman the story, the one she'd planned on telling, about her son, the art director, of his death at age thirty, his short talented life. She walks to her car past the poised mannequins in Santa caps and velvet dresses, past the steps of the church, past the grinning salvation army man with his bells and his magnanimity, "God bless you," even though she hasn't given him a dime, past the caroling children, past a restaurant where sleek young women in worn sweaters clutch coffee mugs and smoke.

He rehydrates his system, forces more water into his body than he can handle, swallows six aspirins, and lays out his corpse on the couch. His head drums the face of the naugahyde cushion. The remote sleeps under his broad flat hand. The hair on that hand is a darkened forest and strangers are hiding in tents beneath the skin.

Dia de los Muertos* by Carol Gloor

The media holiday is immigrant profound,
like the wan, lacy Madonna borne through
1900 Italian streets, only this time
altars to Elvis: seven plastic guitars

and velvet embroidered sideburns.
Or a shrine to two brothers stabbed by gangs:
diplomas, jeans, track shoes,
bags of Oreos, cans of Mountain Dew.

This holiday's right about the one important thing:
the dead do not inhabit graveyards, churches, seances.
They want their stuff.
They miss the only home they ever had.

So, to celebrate Dia de los Muertos,
find the ring he wore for thirty years,
drink tea from that hand painted china cup
she loved, the one with

the black and yellow bird,
rescue his rusty trowel to bury your bulbs,
feel its heft in your hand.
And the dead will rise full-bodied,

like Proust's childhood from his madeleines.
They will rise on Dia de los Muertos.
They will eat your heart.
They have no choice.

*Dia de los Muertos is a traditional Mexican holiday of calling, remem-
bering and honoring the dead, by constructing altars to them of objects
and food they loved.

Monet in Chicago by Carol Gloor

The four water lily paintings in a row
for the first time in a hundred years speak
not only of green noon swelling
to yellow three o'clock, not only

of turquoise six leaching to gray eight,
but also of the patient eyes watching these changes,
of the body brain at rest, awake, under the tree
all afternoon, the only goal: to see.

So may I calm my heart, its endless fears
and lists, and sit a quiet day
by this great lake in the city of my birth,
so may I see how the limbs of swimming children

glisten in the shouting afternoon,
how heat breaks and shimmers across concrete,
how littered Coke cans shine treasure in the sand,
how between noon and eight there are at least

twenty-four shades of blue.

The Night Guido Stopped By by Barbara Govednik

There is a raccoon swaggering down the gangway toward my
apartment wearing a fedora.
He is backlit by the street lamp and the cement beneath his
paws is shiny with rain.
A little cigarette is lit and sticking out from his pointy teeth.
He's walking parallel to the El tracks, just three blocks from a
lake so big
You can't even see the other side.
There is cement and there are trees and there is this raccoon –
each equally out of place.
He manages the steps to my landing not like a quadruped but
smoothly, human.
This raccoon fashions a rope from the twine of my doormat and
Twirls it around his head careful to avoid toppling his hat.
The neighbor's trash is easily lassoed with a tinny clatter.
Henri's Ranch Dressing rolls in ovals towards my door.
Paper containers look like upended toy boats.
The neighbor's garbage can gently sways like an empty cane
rocker
Left out on a warm, sun-bleached porch.
Brown sacks of trash spill egg shells, wrappers, and paper that is
stained dark.
And this raccoon is grazing through the spill.
A soup can has landed upside-down but he can't be bothered to
swipe it over and take a lick.
There are chicken bones at his feet.
He can claw them with the stabs of his toes.
An offering.
Nirvana.
Right on my back porch.

Blue Sky Over the Fjords
by Nancy Hagen

"See my round face and my big wide nose?" Lars Gunnarson asked his daughter one steamy August evening. "That's Norwegian."

He grinned and rolled an ear of corn onto his dinner plate next to two thick slices of beef. Sweat beaded in large drops on his broad forehead.

"Really, Papa?" Kirsten said, smiling back across the table. She and Papa had played this game for years.

"Yah, and see my eyes as bright blue as the sky over the fjords?" Papa continued. "That's Norwegian." He winked at her and pressed his knife into the butter.

Shaking her head, Mama picked up the bowl of mashed potatoes by Kirsten's elbow.

"And look at my hair as brown as a wooden Viking ship!" Papa pointed at his head with his knife. When a clot of butter slid down the blade, he turned it quickly like a juggler keeping a club in the air. "That's Norwegian, too."

"I didn't know that, Papa!" Kirsten giggled, choking on a mouthful of potato.

Ladling more potatoes onto a rose-bordered plate, Mama retorted, "Lars Gunnarson, you were not born in Norway and I was not born in Ireland. This is Chicago and it's 1950. We're all just Americans."

Papa pretended not to hear. "When we were small, Mother read aloud to all five of us kids from her big Norwegian Bible," he said, slathering butter on his corn. "In the winter, Father listened, too, and whittled trolls with big noses or sanded table tops and legs. He made things from wood in Norway, so that's what he did on our farm in Wisconsin, too."

All Kirsten had seen of her grandfather, Olaf Gunnarson, was the silver-framed photograph on Papa's desk: a round-faced young man with a brown handlebar moustache standing in front of a barn door, his hands on the shoulders of a small boy. That was Papa himself, the first of the Gunnarson children.

But Grandpa, who looked so big and strong in the photograph, died when Papa was barely grown and way before Kirsten was born.

"Papa, could I go on the bus to visit Grandma?" Kirsten asked suddenly. "School doesn't start for three weeks."

"That's a good idea, Lars," Mama said. "It would mean a lot to your mother to see more of your only child. And Kirsten is old enough to travel by herself."

Papa frowned and exchanged a long look with Mama.

"Well." He picked up his ear of corn and ate a wide row.

"Good." Mama poked a fork into her mound of potatoes.

* * *

At the noisy bus station downtown a week later, Kirsten hugged Papa and Mama hard. Her legs wobbled when she climbed the steps of the big Greyhound. She wore a light blue sundress with wide straps across the shoulders and her best white sandals. Her braids were pinned across the top of her head to keep her neck cool and make her look grownup. She carried a sack lunch and a small suitcase of her clothes and some presents for Grandma.

Kirsten stared out the bus window the whole way. First she looked at houses and stores and cars, and then at fields of corn and wheat and grazing horses and cows. She was too excited to eat. Her stomach was rumbling when she arrived, some hours later, in a small town near Grandma's farm.

At the bus stop, a tall, red-faced man in farmer overalls said, "It's nice to see you, Kirsten."

"Hello, Uncle Nels," Kirsten said politely.

He picked up her suitcase and they walked to an old black truck at the curb. His fingers were as rough as sandpaper when he gripped her arm to boost her onto the high front seat.

The truck bounced through the town, which was only a few streets long, and out onto a dusty country road. Uncle Nels didn't say anything. Kirsten counted fence posts out the window. Finally, they turned up a rutted lane and stopped in front of a white farmhouse.

After they climbed out of the truck, he said, "Your Grandma's in the kitchen. I'll bring your suitcase in when I've finished the chores." He walked slowly toward the barn that looked the same as in the photograph of Grandpa and Papa. Halfway up the hill behind the barn, brown-and-white cows flicked their tails under a stand of leafy shade trees.

On the farmhouse porch, Kirsten swung open the door calling "Hello!" The hinge creaked and flies buzzed on the screen.

When she stepped inside, the hot kitchen smelled like a bakery. An old woman with a grey bun and pink cheeks was slicing a pie on a black iron stove. A white apron covered the top of her dress.

"Come here my little one!" Grandma exclaimed. Kirsten shyly kissed the wrinkled cheek. Close up, Grandma's eyes were the same color blue as Papa's.

"Now, sit down, child. Sit down and eat! I made it strawberry especially for you!" Grandma put a cream-colored plate with a huge wedge of pie at a place already set with a fork and napkin and a large glass of milk.

"Thank you," Kirsten said. She slid into a chair and awkwardly picked up the fork, which was bigger and heavier than the one she was used to at home. She cut across the point of the pie and lifted the small bite to her mouth. A delicious fruit taste melted on her tongue.

"How pretty you are now, Kirsten, like your Mama," Grandma beamed. Kirsten soon finished the piece of pie and drank the milk. It had been a long time since breakfast in Chicago.

In the following days, Uncle Nels, who didn't have a wife or children, stayed away from the house most of the time. Grandma said he wasn't used to being around strangers.

One by one, Uncle Leif and Uncle Peter and Aunt Olga and Aunt Ingrid came from their nearby farms to ask about Papa and Mama. Kirsten noticed that they didn't look exactly like Papa said all Norwegians did. Uncle Nels' eyes were brown. Uncle Leif's face was as square as a board. The two aunts had blue eyes but long, thin noses. Kirsten soon forgot all that because her aunts and uncles brought her cousins to play.

With Eric and Peter, she ran up and down the long rows of corn and chased the chickens. With Sonja and Dagmar she petted Chester, the horse that was too old to work in the fields, and jumped in the piles of hay in the barn loft.

Still, Kirsten liked to be with Grandma. She would play Old Maid and Go Fish all morning, clap when Kirsten reeled off the Norwegian alphabet Papa had taught her, and tell long stories about the old days on the farm.

The last evening of Kirsten's visit, the two of them nestled on the scratchy brown parlor sofa with the family album. Grandma slowly turned the black paper pages with the pictures held at the corners with little gummed wedges.

"There's your Papa in his baby carriage." Grandma pointed to a small photo on one page.

"He's awfully thin," Kirsten said. She leaned against Grandma's soft shoulder.

"Yes, your father was scrawny as he could be when we brought him home from the orphanage," Grandma agreed.

Kirsten looked up from the photograph. "You mean from the hospital, don't you?"

"Heavens, no. Ladies didn't have their babies in the hospital in my day. I had all my babies at home," Grandma said proudly.

"Then why did you say you brought Papa home from the orphanage?" Kirsten pulled herself up. The back of her legs itched where they'd been pressed to the couch.

"Because that's where Olaf – your Grandpa – and I got him." Grandma looked at her wedding picture next to the couch on the small wood table, a table Grandpa himself had made.

"We were married for four years and still didn't have any children," she sighed, turning to Kirsten. "We decided we may as well start a family by taking a baby who already needed a home."

"Papa was adopted?" Kirsten's heart thumped wildly.

"People didn't talk about such things in those days." Grandma said calmly. She took Kirsten's hand and patted it. "In fact, your Grandpa and I were told your father's people could have been Polish or German or maybe even Irish. Maybe that's why he wanted to marry your Mama." Grandma smiled.

"So Papa's not Norwegian?"

Kirsten pulled her hand away and stood up. Her face was hot. She crossed her arms and tapped her sandals on the braided rag rug in front of the couch.

"How pink your face is, Kirsten! It brings out the blue of your eyes," said Grandma, "a blue like the sky over the fjords."

Another Visit to Cahokia Mounds State Park
by Jane Haldiman

The buried history's echo keeps its beat,
a soundless cleft within the skin of Monk's Mound.
The weeds' impatient gossip at my feet

chafes restless currents up my legs, competes
with wooden stairs that climb and mask the grounds.
The buried history's echo keeps its beat,

the long-gone stockade's fossiled post-holes greet
obscure sun gestures, still wait out its rounds.
The weeds, impatient, gossip at my feet,

weeds gray as interstate inside this heat.
The Gateway Arch across the river frowns.
The buried history's echo keeps its beat,

and keeps time with the summer's buzz, repeats
an earth-encrusted cadence in the sound
of the weeds' impatient gossip at my feet.

An energy circles, always stays complete.
I dutifully pace across the mound.
The buried history's echo keeps its beat
in weeds' impatient gossip at my feet.

Tears for Adam
by Rose Hamilton-Gottlieb

Ginny would rather go straight home from church so she can get out of her girdle and high hells, but Adam turns off the main highway and says, "There's something I want to show you."

They go south in his pickup, past Iowa fields dark and fragrant from the plow, ready for seed. West on gravel, past white farmhouses and red barns. The ruts of a long dirt driveway.

"I know this place. This is your grandparents' farm." She was here once, for Thanksgiving dinner, when his grandparents were alive.

"Was. It's mine now."

"That's great, Adam." She looks at the empty house and feels a tightness in her stomach that has nothing to do with the girdle. Excitement, too. The urge to run toward it and away from it at the same time.

Stepping out of the pickup onto new grass, she says, "You sure you want to be a farmer? You could try something else first. Maybe go to school?" She hasn't told him about her scholarship. Her dreams to teach music. To travel. To live among people.

"The land won't wait," he says simply.

Yes. A farmer's daughter, she knows that. Everything done in its season, and seeds in the ground mean commitment. She knows, too, the pull of the land. But next week she will graduate. Class of 1957. Half her classmates getting married. As if marriage won't wait either.

A burst of lilacs in the front yard. Peony bushes pregnant with buds. Iris thrusting from damp beds. That contagious spring impulse to dig in new earth. She experiments with a feeling of ownership as she picks a lilac sprig and pokes it through his buttonhole. Admires his blond curls, face tan already from outside work.

He smiles and scoops her up, moves to carry her across the threshold, but she laughs and wiggles free. "You'll mess up my new dress."

He looks puzzled at her flimsy excuse, and she's glad when he lets it pass.

They go into the kitchen.

"I'll have to mend that screen. Cats clawed it."

He opens windows while she stands uncertainly in the middle of the square room. Her kitchen, if she wants. A twinge of excitement.

He struggles with a swollen window frame, gives up. "I'll fix that when I get time."

Mustard colored linoleum. A sink with a drainboard. Battered table. Marble topped washstand.

"Kind of old fashioned," he apologizes, "but someday I'll put in a new sink with hot water. He gestures toward a cabinet. "Get rid of this old stuff and build cupboards. This winter if it's a good year."

The wringer washing machine crouches in a corner of the back porch, which looks out on the garden.

"I'll plow the garden next week. Want to help me plant seeds?"

"Sure." Sees them set out tomato seedlings together. But she doesn't do what she wants, which is to kick off her shoes and clean the weeds from around his grandmothers's strawberry plants. That would make them hers, and she's not sure she wants that. Not yet.

The root cellar. The fenced-in areas with the chicken house and the smaller brooder house. She retreats to the kitchen, then through it to the empty front room.

She remembers crocheted antimacassars pinned to the backs of chairs and on the piano nobody played. Sold at auction with the other furniture. Thinks of her music scholarship to Simpson College. Do scholarships wait?

She remembers she likes the order of this house, felt embarrassment at her own mother's disorder and flurries of emergency cleaning when unexpected company pulled into the driveway. Colliers and Post magazines everywhere. Piles of library books.

She never saw a book here, just Kitchen Klatter magazines in a rack, and she wonders if Adam's grandmother awakened after her stroke, her crocheting fingers paralyzed, to realize she had never seen a mountain or the ocean. At least her mother read about them.

Dead flies on window sills, a dusty flowered rug, threadbare in places.

"I'll put down wall-to-wall carpet someday."

Scratched hardwood floor in the dining room.

"In here, too."

Adam hangs his tie on the banister, unbuttons his collar and starts up steep, narrow stairs. She follows. Warning bells go off in her mind, but her body sings in response to their footsteps in collusion on the steep, dark stairs. On the landing, he turns to kiss her, long and deep. The kiss ends and her lips reach the hollow of his throat. His pulse there. His chest hair on her chin. His Adam smell beneath the aftershave.

He leads her up three more steps to a small, sun-filled room. "Grandma's sewing room." He opens a door at the far end. "This was their bedroom. Gets the south breeze. I want to show you something."

He opens the closet door and pulls a dangling string. A dim light bulb reveals the musty interior. He points upward. "Square nails," he says proudly. "That proves the house is really old." He slaps the wall with the flat of his hand. "She's well built, though. Survived a lot of storms."

She nods in appreciation, but wrinkles her nose and backs out. "Smells like mice in here."

He opens a window. Smells of damp earth and new grass. Outside, an oak is about to burst into tiny explosions of green. Beyond it, the barn and smaller outbuildings. He wraps his arms around her from behind and pulls her close. She leans into him.

"That's the hog house, over there." he says.

She sees the identical building, at home, with one whole wall hacked away. It was the winter after her father died. Spying on her mother, that day after school, as she chopped at the hog house with the axe, a pile of splintered boards at her feet, overshoes mired in mud. Strangled sobs. Afterward, her mother came in and cooked supper, as if nothing had happened, but every day, the hog house shrank until one whole wall was gone. By then it was spring and time to plant. Why did she do it? Why did this one building absorb the blows of her mother's grief and rage and disappointment?

She turns in his arms, wills him to forget, for the moment, the hog house and to not name all the fields, which she knows he's about to do. His cheek is smooth and hot against hers. Old Spice.

He makes a sound that comes from somewhere deep and pulls her against the whole length of him. Then, still kissing her, down onto the dusty rug.

Her shoes slip off. Still kissing her, he caresses her body, inches up her skirt, runs his fingers over the fabric at the top of her nylons. Unsnaps one garter. "Oh, Amy," he groans, and half covers her body with his.

She's used to him in stiff blue jeans on the cramped car seat, parked in front of the house, or at the drive-in movie. Always the danger of others close by. Here, on the rug, under the white shirt and thin fabric of his dress pants, his body is fluid and free and there is no one to stop them. He strokes her bare thigh, finds the top of her girdle. She moves with him.

But the girdle balks, clings to her damp flesh like a second skin with no nerve endings. A gift of time to think. This isn't the back seat of his dad's car; they're alone in an empty house. His house. Well, so what? Maybe she will marry him. Hasn't he been asking her by showing her through this house with the square nails and so much fixing up in its future? Asking her to be the woman who will hoe the garden and traipse up and down the root cellar fifty times a day for the next hundred years? Who will stand at the linoleum-covered work table and roll out a thousand rounds of pie crust while she looks out at the road to see if anyone is coming to see her?

She's always known she would be married, since that day when she was seven, watching her mother at her work table. "Mama, I don't think I'll get married when I grow up," she said, testing the water to see what was possible.

Mama put down her rolling pin, turned on her. "Don't you dare to be an old maid."

Maybe she *will* be an old maid if she doesn't marry Adam.

She's about to help him with the girdle when he gives up to unbutton her blouse. That's safe and familiar. She opens her mouth to his tongue. Moves experimentally against him. He fumbles again with the girdle. Yes, she will marry him. If she does this, they'll be engaged for sure, and she wants this. Yes, just this, forever.

But dust from the rug tickles her nose, makes her sneeze. She sneezes again as dust swirls in the dirty shaft of sunlight slanting through the window. She sits up and sneezes once more and looks out at the hog house surrounded by mud.

He tries to pull her back down, but now her head is clear. "Adam, no." Tempers it with "not now," her voice as shaky as she feels.

"Ginny, please," he says hoarsely. "We're going to be married, aren't we? After graduation?" He reaches for her, but there, before her, lies the hog house. The dirt road. The empty fields. A terrible grief rises, and she cries, and can't tell him her tears are for him.

Carcasses (An excerpt)
by Patricia Herczfeld

This man doesn't deserve poems
and they shouldn't be given to him in any form.
His poems, should he ever produce any more,
ought to be eaten by mice.
                    — Raymond Carver

There were times when the desire to write was so strong, it would cut through the weariness that clung to most of her days. One evening when Brian fell asleep on the couch, Casia took the remote from his hands and sped through the channels looking for something, anything that would stop her from thinking. Then she heard the words rise in the air like an incantation. The picture was blurred, that wiggly pattern from a restricted station, a ban for nonpaying eyes. She did not need the picture to know the voice: clipped, precise, delivering a volley of diamond-cut words. Plath. Casia sat unmoving, mouthing the words in cadence with the voice emanating from the television, words dredged up from memory.

That night she was the only one awake. The children were asleep. Brian, after their lovemaking, fell into that untroubled sleep reserved for those who work long hours out of doors, those who use their bodies so completely, no worry can pull them back to wakefulness. She went to the kitchen to have one more cigarette before giving in to another restless night.

There was no need to turn on the light: the enamel of the stove and refrigerator glowed in the moonlight. It had been a late fall. Summer lingered and played with autumn. Only now in the final weeks of October did the chill assert itself. Despite the chill, she did not want to stay inside. Casia stepped out on the porch and felt the wind on her skin, still damp from the lovemaking. It was not a long distance from the porch to the row of birch trees at the back of the yard. It was those trees that made her decide this is where she would live. The other house, the one her sister said she was crazy to pass up, had a finished basement, a gas grill, and a smooth carpet of grass with orderly shrubs on either side. But this house had trees that swayed with the wind, as though dancing before the moon. She walked between those trees as she did that first year. Pregnant with Timmy then, she had claimed sleeplessness when in truth she walked at night beneath the trees to speak out loud the lines that had formed in her mind throughout the day.

Tonight the memories of those days, simple and hopeful, no longer seemed as though they belonged to someone else. Above her, the wind rifled the silver leaves that still clung to the birches. The branches parted and revealed the moon, tatters of clouds passing before its face. Casia let the robe slip to the ground, as wind brushed against throat, breasts and thighs. When the wind stopped, the leaves on the ground gave up their scent, fecund and rich.

As she walked naked beneath the moon, words and phrases took shape in her mind, like the faceless people of a dream who slowly acquire eyes and mouths. When she gathered her robe to return to the house she looked around for her cigarette, then realized she had never lit it.

At the kitchen table she tore a sheet from Timmy's penmanship notebook, the yellow paper lined for the A's and B's that would march like eager young cadets. She wrote the octet of a sonnet, eight lines tied by one metaphor. Not perfect, but she could work on that tomorrow. And the sextet? That would come to her too. She returned to bed for a sleep as deep as Brian's.

* * *

The next day Mary Jo called and told her that Rebecca had resigned from the committee ("Too much to do, as though she's the only one!") and asked, would Casia, please, please, take over the spring raffle? After all, didn't she want Timmy's school to have the best? Casia said yes, she would get the job done. But as she hung up the phone, she felt the weariness seep back into her arms, legs and head.

Weeks later she found the unfinished sonnet in the pocket of her robe, after it had been washed. The paper was soft and nappy, the writing blurred illegibly, except for a few blue letters that stood their ground on a field of yellow. Casia took the paper and placed it inside an envelope which contained other scraps of paper, even dinner napkins, with words and phrases written, crossed out, rewritten.

*   *   *

That night she had a dream.

She was driving on old County Road A on a grey, cold morning. A small animal shot into the road in front of her car. In her rearview mirror she saw the body roll and roll onto the roadside gravel. Casia got out of the car and walked back to the body. The creature looked as though it was sleeping, paws pulled close together, the way her fat tabby curled up for a nap in the sun. The fur was a pale brown, tipped in black, with streaks of red. It might have been a young raccoon, but its face was fetal, unformed, as though it had ventured out of the nest before its time. The legs looked abnormally short. No wonder it couldn't make it across the road.

Back in her car she looked at the fuel gauge. No gas. How had she let it get so low? She'd never make it to Mary Jo's house. Not even to the Amoco in town.

Then she saw the sign that said "Gas." An old sign, bereft of brand names, as though gas was a necessity, like water, or truth. Something you couldn't live without. Something that would do the job no matter who claimed to manufacture it, package it. Something so necessary you'd take it from anybody's hands.

She had passed this abandoned station so many times. The pumps were antiques, signposts of a time when city families climbed into their cars and drove just to enjoy a day in the country. Behind the pumps was a shack that survived the seven winters and summers she had lived in town. What lived inside the shack, what insects and animals called it home?

Today there were signs of life other than animal. The door of the shack was open; someone moved inside. She pulled the car into the station, looking for the side of the pump that announced "Self Serve." There was no such sign, nor did the pump announce a brand name. What was this, some moonshine gas? She hoped that it wouldn't eat up the insides of her car.

As the car crossed the air hose, she expected to hear the familiar "ping-ping," but there was silence. A man came out of the shack, someone she did not recognize from town. He was tall and wore faded blue overalls and a baseball cap of the same material. A beard covered the lower half of his face, a nest of brown and black streaked with red hair. It was not a trimmed beard, but one that climbed in patches up his pale, bony cheeks. His eyes were very dark and shiny, even bright, like the water of the river at night and just as cold.

"Morning, ma'am. What'll it be?" the voice was higher than she expected and somehow off-key.

"Ten gallons of premium, please."

"We have but one kind."

"Well, I guess I'll take that."

As the man fed the gas into the tank, Casia tried to get a better look at him in the side view mirror. When she leaned forward to center his image in the mirror, there was his reflection, grinning at her, his lips lifted off uneven teeth.

She knew it was safer to stay put, to be able to start the car in an instant if she needed to. There was a tightening then a rush in her chest, and she began to hear the pounding of the blood in her ears. She tried to get another look at the man in her mirror, but suddenly he was in front of her, washing the windshield with a squeegee and rag. He left the window grimier than before, but he was not looking at the glass. With the same grin he continued to look at her through the windshield.

Then man stood by the driver's window and said, "That's fifty dollars."

Ridiculous, she thought, for no-name gas. She reached for her wallet then stopped. Something almost perverse made her turn and face the man at her window.

"Tell me something. I've been noticing these small animals trying to cross the highway in broad daylight. I thought they were night creatures. What are they?"

Still grinning, the man shrugged, "What does it matter? They weren't good enough to survive."

The answer chilled her, and irritated too.

"You didn't answer my question. I asked you what are they?"

The man laughed and placed his hands on the door. They were thin, pale, the nails stained with dried blood. When he folded them over the rim onto the upholstery inside, all eight fingers were the exact, same length.

"Well, I'm surprised you didn't recognize them. They're your poems, ma'am."

She turned on the ignition and shifted the car into drive. It lurched as she floored the accelerator and screeched into the road. When the car straightened from its skid, she did not have enough time to stop before another animal dashed from the culvert into the road. She hit it and sat up in bed as the vomit rose in her throat.

Fallow
by Joyce Hinnefeld

"In the woods around her the invisible cricket choruses had struck up, but what she heard were the voices of the souls climbing upward into the starry field and shouting hallelujah."

— Flannery O'Connor, **Revelation**

When the wind blew through the dry, papery leaves of the woods behind the high school, a chorus of cicadas joined the rising, swelling wave of late-summer sound. Anne Louise Bowman held her breath, let her chest cave in with the weight until the wave subsided, rolled back, a moment's reprieve before the next round of hot, dry wind and singing insects.

She breathed out into the silence. Later, surely, there would be a storm – rain at last, release.

She smiled at the image of a wave, here in this flat valley, this landlocked Midwestern prairie worlds away from any ocean or sea. She stared out the window of her empty classroom at the burnt brown grass. When the cicadas trilled again, it was as if each blade of grass had somehow found a voice and cried out in the agony of this three o'clock August heat.

She had just finished rereading Flannery O'Connor's *Revelation*. Her pulse beat faster and faster, as it always did, as she read up to the critical moment, the letting loose, the flying free of a clenched spring – when ugly, acne-ridden Mary Grace from Wellesley College lets fly the Human Development book, striking Mrs. Turpin square above her left eye. And then, her fateful, clear-eyed whisper: "Go back to hell where you came from, you old wart hog."

Anne Louise imagined saying this to Barbara Stevens, the typing teacher, who did in fact resemble a wart hog and whose smug, self-righteous image she always drew on when she pictured Mrs. Turpin. Or better yet, from the back row of the bandroom, at the dreadful beginning-of-the-year faculty meeting, slamming shut her Harbrace English Handbook and throwing it with might and finesse, watching it curve in a graceful arc above the rows of impassive music stands and bland backs of teachers' heads, before connecting, perfectly, with the shiny left temple of the principal, Mr. Hodges. Just to the inside of his dark brown sideburn, which, when seen in profile, looked disturbingly like the left sideburn of her husband, John.

John was a principal, too, but at a different school – a larger one in a wealthier town, 20 miles away. He was a coach as well – esteemed, beloved, at home in his world in a way Anne Louise knew she would never be.

The cicadas sang out in loud, ascending unison. Just when she thought the sound might make her cry or make her mad, it died away again.

Every year at this time, she read *Revelation* again and toyed, briefly, momentarily intoxicated by the notion, with the idea of assigning the story to her twelfth grade students. And this year, as every year before, her initial excitement faded as she imagined the reactions of these students – children, all of them, of parents who were perfect clones of Claud and Ruby Turpin, the hog-farming couple at the center of O'Connor's story.

That is to say – the wind swelled and her heart and stomach sank as she thought of it – they wouldn't understand, they'd see no reason to react at all when Ruby Turpin wonders to herself what, if Jesus forced her to pick, she would choose to be: a nigger or white trash.

They would have an intuitive sense of what was meant by "white trash," some of them. Except for the ones who belonged, undeniably, in that category themselves. "Nigger" would make some of them giggle, others squirm in their seats.

Someone would complain to Mr. Hodges, who would object, in his usual ignorance, to the use of such labels. If he bothered to read the story at all, if he even grasped any of it, he would find it troubling in its ambiguity about spiritual matters.

That would be his assessment of Flannery O'Connor. Troubling. And therefore bad.

The truth was, the story seemed to her to reach its climax there in the middle, in the scene in the doctor's waiting room, when Mary Grace bursts furiously into Ruby Turpin's narrow-minded, hog-filled world. The truth was, as far as Anne Louise was concerned, the story could have ended there. She knew the real "revelation" was supposed to come at the end, with Ruby Turpin's strange vision, of pigs and hogs and niggers and white trash and people like herself, all together at last, all ascending the long stairs up to heaven. And she knew that if she ever actually assigned the story, she'd have to deal with that oddly uplifting image at the end.

But that was just Flannery O'Connor's Catholicism getting in the way of a good story, as far as Anne Louise was concerned. For her, the most glorious moment came square in the middle, with that leveling blow to the old hypocrite's temple, and the hissing, whispered advice to her to go back to hell where she came from.

A broom brushed by her open door, reminding her of the hour. The custodians were cleaning, though there wasn't yet any noticeable dirt, sweeping the air in the empty halls. The other teachers would be gone by now, football practice starting up. Classes were to start the next week, the first football game was set for that Friday, and there wasn't even a hint, not the slightest smell, of fall in the air.

The ground and the leaves were the burnt brown-yellow of late summer. Their color made her dizzy, and a little nauseated. John would expect dinner promptly at 6:00, even though she'd gone back to work as well. But there should be time enough for cooking, as they didn't have a child. As that had not happened, and would not happen now. As some part of her, something deep within her, would keep her womb an arid plain as visible to her mind's eye as the brown grass outside her classroom window.

In the end, Mrs. Turpin saw the souls of pigs and hogs climbing the long, steep stairs to heaven. Pigs and hogs,"a-gruntin and a-rootin and a-groanin" in the words of the white trash girl in the waiting room, the one who thanked "Gawd" she wasn't a pig. Or a nigger.

Anne Louise searched in her bag for her car keys before stepping out into the blinding afternoon. In the parking lot the sun beat down on the hot new asphalt; it looked soft enough to sink in, and it smelled strongly of oil. The bright yellow lines that marked the empty spaces stung her tired eyes, causing her to squint.

The lines were new this year. Last spring, on the last day of school for the seniors, Mike Eckard – one of her favorite students because of his unfailing irreverence – had led a handful of other seniors in a small rebellion. They parked their cars every which way in the parking lot – some backwards, some at odd angles. Mike's pick-up truck was parked sideways, square in the middle of the front row, which was reserved for teachers. In its back window was large white poster board with the message, "You give us no lines, no direction. How are we supposed to know where we should be?"

There was a tense stand-off between Mike and Mr. Hodges the whole morning, delaying the annual honors assembly for two hours, until finally, at 10:30, Mike and the others put their cars back in neat, tidy rows at the back of the lot, all pointing respectfully toward the school. It might have gone on longer if several of the young rebels hadn't had to get to their 1:00 shifts at the paper mill that afternoon.

The teachers, of course, were expected to maintain a grave, tight-lipped countenance in response to the "crisis," saying nothing. And Anne Louise had complied, except for a brief, appreciative chuckle – that roused an angry glare from Barbara Stevens – with her friend Susan, who taught health and human development, in the teachers' lounge earlier that morning. But later, at the honors assembly, she made a point of catching Mike's eye as he passed her row during the seniors' procession and giving him a small, approving nod.

Now Mike worked in a factory on the edge of the town where John was the happy high school principal. Mike's young wife was pregnant. This, of course, was why she was his wife instead of his girlfriend, which would make more sense for two people as young as they were, as Anne Louise knew. Mike couldn't afford college on his own, and his parents could see no reason for him to go. The guidance counselor decided his high test scores didn't mean much when you considered what a bad attitude he had.

"How are we supposed to know where we should be?"

"A-gruntin and a-rootin and a-groanin . . ."

Driving home, Anne Louise drove over the little bridge above Sugar Creek, normally a wide, circling stream with tiny waterfalls shining brilliant in the sun, but now, in this unforgiving August heat, a dry bed of cracked gray mud. As she had that morning on her way in to school, she pulled over to the side of the road and walked down to the edge of the creek bed, below the bridge. She looked for what she'd left there that morning – a little pool of vomit in the shadow of the bridge – and found it soon enough. The midday sun had reached it, drying it, making it nearly indistinguishable from the powdery mud it lay in, save for the little flecks of yellow egg, angry vestiges of the breakfast her body had refused.

There was no shade, no relief anywhere, and she stood there in the pounding sun until she felt as if she were swimming, circling in waves of a thick liquid heat. The cicadas were screaming furiously, directly into her ear; their voices rose and rose, never falling, never pausing for breath. She thought that they might leave her deaf.

At last she drove home without the air conditioner, soaking quietly, unmoving, in a sheath of her own sweat. Home, where she would wait, quiet and still, for the rain that she knew would never come.

Time and Distance
by Jen Hinton

Karen wanted her money.

"My mother's been up in my face for five months now," she said. "You all both know I don't have a job and I don't need the aggravation."

"Karen, where on earth have you been?" I was miffed. She hadn't been returning my calls in weeks.

Karen said she had other concerns. Her mother had been riding her for a huge phone bill we had no business running up that spring while we were both away at college. One call in particular lasted the course of an entire night.

Looking back on that night, maybe we should've picked up pens as we usually did, rather than phone receivers; but that spring, it seemed events were running so far ahead of words that we didn't feel best of friends should have to answer to time and distance.

And friends were running in very short supply on our respective campuses. In these new worlds, friends changed the subject when you worried about your father's health. Friends kept one eye on the television when you agonized about low grades or philandering boyfriends or careers. So we turned to each other, even across 500 miles.

The spark that ignited the marathon phone call was Karen's break up with Ray. Their last battle, over his girlfriends back in Cincinnati, ended with Ray slapping Karen and Karen whacking him with a Chemistry book.

"Guess it's over now," Karen kept repeating as if there still could have been some doubt left.

We talked about guys for a long time, then our call segueued to discussions of classwork, the bathrooms in Europe, recipes for pound cake, the cholesterol scam, stuck-up sorority girls, careers, her father's gun collection, the church of Ronald Reagan, Prince vs.

Hendrix, guys, my grandmother's moth balls and the time a bat flew out of her closet, tornado preparedness, a Marxist interpretation of the White Sox-Cubs rivalry and the implications of a subway World Series, being alone vs. being lonely, and how every time we saw a Greyhound bus, we looked at the sign on the front to see where it was headed.

This monster call alone came to $58. At first, Karen promised to take care of the bill. She planned to come home from Wisconsin, find a summer job and pay back her mother with her first check. But after searching for three weeks without any job interviews, she was coming up short.

"Can't you borrow against your loan?" I wondered.

"My loan situation is completely fucked up. Guess what: When you owe $5000, they don't let you register."

"Five thousand? Karen, what happened?"

"*He* never came up with the money in October. (Karen never referred to her father as "Dad" or "my father." She used the pronoun because they were strangers). *He* says he doesn't have it – Mr. BMW."

"Five thousand, what are you going to do?"

She gave a chilly laugh. "Nothing. At least not back at UW anyway."

"Why didn't you tell me sooner? Jesus, Karen. I'm sorry – "

"I don't need your 'sorry,' I need your help here. Can I get that $58?"

"Okay, let's meet somewhere Saturday. Then we can go to the show."

"You don't seem to be hearing me. I don't have any 'Let's go to the show' money."

"I can treat."

"Will you just bring that $58? Soon?"

"Yeah...what about Tuesday, after I get off work?"

"Wonderful...At least someone's working."

* * *

When I wish to think back, I remember how Karen and I first became friends. Angela, Jeannette and Karen had been meeting for lunch just as nicely all semester. I ate with Ronica and Lisa, two girls from my gym class who couldn't swim either. Then one day after

New Year's, Angela and Jeannette were tapped to join the LDJs (Les Dames Jeunes) – the girls who drove and carried Coach bags, whose fathers were dentists or high school principals – and Karen came over to our table cursing about "those snotty tramps." It cracked us up because she was so *loud*. Anyone could hear. Marcus was right behind us standing in the juice line. Surely, he would tell his friend Leo, who'd tell his girlfriend Sandra, who'd tell her sister Meredith, the LDJ treasurer. At the time, we thought the LDJs had so much power. The audacity of someone not to give a shit.

This is how we choose our friends. We sit together in the cafeteria.

Although I'd known Karen since my freshman year in high school, I'd never been to or even seen her home. She lived in an area on the West Side she said was called "K-Town" because all the street names began with "K". But our high school and my home were both on the South Side, so we end up hanging out on the South Side and at my house. In this way, Karen was pretty much a South Sider as well. My opinion was the world was a ghetto; but once, Ronica and Lisa got going about the "Wild" West Side and Karen popped her cork very quickly.

"I may be from the 'hood, but I am not *of* it," she said heatedly. "Home is *not* an address, but a state of mind."

I didn't really understand, but it seemed like something sort of religious. So I just nodded like I did every day in the geometry class I almost flunked that semester.

* * *

Although the South Side where I lived had its share of blighted areas, there was something about the travelling clear across town, the gradual transformation from familiar streets to unfamiliar, from "our" ghetto to "theirs," the roaming alone with no one knowing where I was, that had me thinking maybe I wasn't up to returning the $58 as I stepped off the bus.

Karen's address was a huge, mustard-yellow building spray-painted with gang graffiti on a long, dark block of awesome buildings sprayed with gang markings. This was where the phone I'd rung so many nights all through high school was picked up by Karen.

A handful of people gathered by the doorway.

As I approached, two men walked to the gate and guarded either side. On any side of town, this meant trouble. One man's face was like a werewolf with his thick lambchop sideburns, beard, dense afro and heavy eyebrows.

"Where you going?" He asked.

"Karen Smith's," I answered quickly.

"Where she stay at?"

For some reason, I felt I shouldn't lie. Like it wouldn't make a difference. "Apartment 4D."

"Real?"

I nodded.

"Is any of ya'll know some Karen Smith?"

I heard what I hoped was backfire from a bus.

"They the ones just move in?" A short, bowlegged woman with piercings around her entire earlap, piped up.

"Who they?"

"They six of 'em," she said. "They them ones don't never come out. Kinda stuck up?"

The man nodded and thought about this for awhile. I was making up my mind as well: to mail Karen her damn $58; when slowly, he uncrossed his arms and opened the gate.

"Shit, as long as they mind they own business and don't fuck with my play, we straight."

"Thank you," I uttered, stepping very gingerly past him to avoid somehow insulting his diplomacy.

It was like nighttime in Karen's stairwell. At 4D, I rang and Karen answered her door. She looked different from when I'd last seen her. She wasn't fatter or skinnier or anything. I couldn't put my finger on it, but I could tell she was in no mood to discuss silly old things like school, boys or music.

"Well, you made it," she said, sounding surprised.

I handed her the money.

"Thanks."

The earring woman outside was cursing and carrying on.

"I can use this."

I couldn't move.

"Can't you talk anymore? What's wrong with you?"

"I think I need to get out of here. It's getting dark...I'm afraid."

She clicked and unclicked the deadbolt lock. "Don't you think I feel the same way?"

"About what?"

Karen abruptly stopped fidgeting with the lock. Her lips parted but no words came out. Her eyes looked stunned.

"Well," she said slowly, "let me let you go then." But she just remained there, waiting.

I felt ill.

"I'm sorry – "

She raised her hand in a "stop" position. "Go home." She shrugged. "I'll call you."

I nodded, "Yeah."

As soon as I stepped away, the door closed. Shut with no reverb. The stairwell was dark and silent. When I emerged onto the dim, evening street, the gang had moved on down the block.

*   *   *

During that summer, our calls became more and more infrequent and shorter and shorter. Karen finally found a job with UPS and really became involved in that. She said she was anyway. Soon, our calls were just missing one another.

Then one day after I'd gone back to college, I called and their number had been disconnected. Around that time, my letters to that address were being returned. Karen had never mentioned that they were moving.

This is how we lose our friends. We just walk away.

Of course and naturally, I realize now what I had with Karen, what her last words meant, what I just threw out like litter. With Karen, I had a place of complete safety and trust. I could let it all hang loose. Kick off my shoes. With her, I had what she had defined all those years ago as a home. And without Karen, all these years now, I've been, in a sense, homeless.

At My Mother's Sink
by Kay Jordan

Mother washed, I dried and in the next room Father sat, bathed in television blue. He never asked what we talked about all those nights, all those years at my mother's sink.

1959

Rainbows steam; white suds mountain.

"Today the teacher took my book," I complain. "The boys have been reading dirty books with paper backs, so she said no soft-bound books allowed. But mine was Ellery Queen."

Mother plunges a glass beneath the soapy surface, says sharply, "You knew the rule?"

I twist, untwist the towel. Through the open kitchen door I see Father's head eclipse the TV's vacuum glow. I nod.

Mother repeats, "You knew the rule, and you broke it." Splashing suds, she sings a silly song, as if a victory has been won.

1965

I dry three knives, a spoon and ask, "Why didn't you go to college?"

A shrug. "No money."

I dry two spoons, then say, "Uncle Joe went to college."

"He was the son."

In the next room Fred Flintstone yells "Yabba dabba doo." Father laughs.

We finish the flatware before I venture, "If you had gone to college . . ."

Mother lifts her soapy hand. Bubbles dissolve, are gone. "I would have flown away."

1972

"And after the wedding, Larry wants – "

Mother attacks a plate. Water slops from the sink.

I slam a cupboard door. "Mother, what *is* your problem with this wedding?"

"The problem with *all* weddings," her voice stings; her eyes snap, "is that they end in marriage."

"Would you two be quiet!" Father shouts. "I want to hear the latest news from Viet Nam."

Mother bows her head, stills her working hands. "So many women lose their lives to love. And no one notices that they have died."

1980

I dry a pot too vigorously, announce too gaily, "Come Thanksgiving you'll be a grandma again."

Mother scours a skillet with S.O.S. "Will your novel be finished?"

Canned laughter drifts from Father's television.

"No, but . . . we'll work something out."

"About writing, you mean?"

I hang the pot in its proper place. "Besides, children are worth a few sacrifices. Aren't they?"

"Of course they are!" Mother drowns the skillet in brown sudsless water. "You kids were all I had."

1990

I hang up the wet dishtowel, say unsteadily, "Larry will have custody of the kids. It's for the best. The boys need their father."

Mother nods, wipes the counter with a damp sponge.

"He's buying my share of the house."

Mother rinses the sponge, wipes the spotless counter again.

"I have to write, but I couldn't work, couldn't think. Not with everyone. Everything. Every day."

In the next room a contestant spins the Wheel of Fortune. Father cheers.

Mother glances in his direction. "Have you told him?"

"He ranted and raged. When he ran out of breath, I said, 'It's my life.'"

Mother pulls the plug and watches the dirty water drain away. "I'm thinking of buying a dishwasher," she says. "I've saved enough, you know."

Fallen Angels by Marcia Karlin

*The May 25, 1995, Pioneer Press reported that unknown vandals
destroyed several life-sized sculptures at the Techny religious
retreat...and attacked the female swan nesting on the pond there,
beating her with a broken statue of Jesus Christ, blinding her,
destroying her seven eggs, and ending her life...Swans mate for life.*

Sculpted saints watch in silence among willows and reborn daffodils
Constant companions as she tends her nest, though
    others come and go,
pause to admire Kabuki eyes and sinuous neck
scrolling sublimely over ivory wings.

Alone at night behind fastened gates, floating in her moon-filled pond,
she dreams of promises kept in the vault of a cloistered shell.
Until the crack of fractured stone splits the blossoming air,
bringing stone saints to their knees in silent, hopeless prayer.
Blinking at a trembling moon, shattered in the pond
    like a porcelain plate,
she dreams dark angels rising from the gaping mirror.
Gargoyle faces split with laughter, hurling relics of the broken Christ
toward her ebony eyes. And her world turns cold and black,
though the moon still clings to a starless sky.

Battered and blinded by fallen angels, distorted reflections of Gabriel
bringing news of a holy child, she leaves a plundered nest to her mate.
He mourns his winged madonna, joined by saints reduced to rubble
and willows bent to weep into a blood-stained pond.

South Manitou Island by Susanna Lang

In the Chippewa story the dune's a bear
who sleeps, and waits for the two cubs
she'd led away from the hungry fire.
They cannot come; they're rooted now,
two islands in the bay. Asleep
it seems she's barely there, her shape
eroded by the wind that buries
trees in sand, her heart picked clean
by waves that wash against her sides.

The old road through the dunes is bright
with flowers brought here casually
by European settlers: sweet
white clover, Queen Annes lace, and purple
knapweed with its thistle leaves;
flowers that grow in fields left empty
by the farmers who move on.
Those who stay plant rows of trees
that tame the inland hills and bend
with loads of fruit for markets far
from here. Yet close to shore the sand
still shifts, and native plants take hold
—the beachgrass, sandreed, little bluestem,
beach pea, wormwood and the broomrape—
holding out against the constant
wind. And then, on dunes the books
call "stabilized," the berry bushes
named for bear and buffalo,

the cottonwood that almost can
outgrow the advancing sand. But stands
of whitened trunks like ghosts remind
us that the wind will win, the shore
fall back upon itself, the sand
move inland and the grasses fail.

From the ferry the coast looks empty
of all but trees and sand. The settlers
saw a virgin land, and took
it for themselves, convinced that God
had meant all virgins to conceive.
Yet now where fields are left, the trees
grow back, and we stand back to watch
the tug of war of wind and grass
along the dunes. Today we'll walk
this island, smaller of the two
the Spirit placed here (goes the tale)
to mark the place where two cubs drowned,
while up above their mother sleeps
and guards the land, a few years more.

The Landscape of My Life
by Anne H. Massaro

Leftover leaves of fall
blow across the bare fields.
Drifts pile high,
then the wind sweeps by
leaving dark patches of nothingness.

Dry, brittle twigs still poke through,
their life-giving sap motionless
beneath the ground -
frozen in icy stillness.

The sun now casts its warmth.
Diamond-like sparkles lay on the snow covered land.
Slowly,
slowly,
a melting begins...

Angela's Folly Bloomed for Easter by Kathy Mayer

A thick ground cover in green and silver,
its variegated leaves stay green all winter,
then pop out in puffy purple blooms for spring.
It flowers until well into November, this
optimistic, hardy plant touched with grace
so like my Aunt Angela herself.

She named it unintentionally one summer.
As visiting nieces toured the yard with her,
an after-supper tradition, she pulled a weed now and then,
steadying her stoop by holding on to one of their arms.

"Oh, heavens, I've forgotten what it's called,"
she had laughed when one of them asked the name
of the plant she trimmed from its wanderings.

She'd planted it fifty or sixty years earlier,
before her hair matched the silver in its leaves.
"I call it my folly because it's taken over everywhere."

Not quite everywhere, for these nieces
were just getting their first starts of it.
A few plantings with roots dangling from moist black soil,
shoveled into cardboard boxes and packed into the car
along with her gentle reminder to "Be happy."

Angela's Folly headed south that day,
soon to bloom at new homes. And from those yards to more
as her nieces' friends asked, "What's that purple flower," then
found themselves headed home
with a bit of Angela's Folly.

I first spotted this year's blooms
on a rolling wooded farm in Carroll County, Indiana.
A place Angela never visited, people she never knew.
Her Folly had been passed on by a niece
to artists who added Angela's purple to the pallet
of their creek-side studio.

Although she had died a year earlier,
Angela was there in comfortable elegance on Easter day,
a welcoming spirit chuckling in joyous familiarity.

A friend once told me she thought she knew
the plant's real name.
I told her I already knew it.

Surviving the Heat by Ethney McMahon

she just did it:
jumped off the bridge
on I-94
down and out.
just like that
free-falling
for five seconds
into bumpers
and horns

bearing down
into a convoy
of death:

she hits me
head on

as i watch
a boy hold the head
of a hydrant
between his legs

spraying the children
whose bodies
sparkle brave
on the pavement

in this heat
of a Chicago
June

Woman Dead in Wicker Park by Ethney McMahon

chicago, 4th of july

like a detective
i follow myself into the truck
and south on Damen

driving slowly by the park
everyone looks guilty

and someone
is shooting fireworks
over the lake

i think
the way they go off
is
the way
you went out

burning in fear
naked and alone

i don't know the way
to your
name

you could have been one
of 100 dead bodies cut

o p e n
all over the city

aiming the light
that split open

the
s k y

Prairie Hearts

Hawk Season by Gwyn McVay

Eagle Creek Dam, Indiana

The human eye spots inconsistencies – breaks
in the scrub and trees, a ripple of ice
where floodlights fall from a dam, a hunched body
high on the rim of a dam. The tongue supplies names –
red-tail, sharp-shin – but falls silent in the cold,
that stealing hour before dawn when the frost splinters
with subtle cracks, and the hawk shakes out its wings,
stoops, and rises. The lights on Eagle Creek
break and scatter. All that a human can see
to name is a silhouette – buteo, accipiter.

Being Deconstructed by Karla Linn Merrifield

Whatever happened to that poet?
I heard her long-time lover
moved away
some place warmer
a land drier
a state where the seasons do not
change to challenge the soul.
To Phoenix, Arizona, I think
he went and took a better job.

Whatever happened to our poet?
I guess her would-be lover
walked away
with a case of spiritual paralysis.
He was simply afraid
to just frankly taste her
power, the promise of unfolding cycles
so familiar to life in Western New York
where he could not risk losing his job.

Whatever happened to her?
Reportedly she burned out, dried up
one frustratingly barren autumn night.
With no inspiring Muse to savor, she merely
wandered away.
We believe it was out there, nowhere
in the flat, blank Midwest
that she joined the other unemployed poets
and died, dear God, a little more.

She Who Wears the Pants

by Lee Mirand

I could tell Mom was upset about something. I pressed my nose against the kitchen screen door to get a better look. Her thin, dark eyebrows were knotted over the creases in her forehead. One grey clump from her perfectly styled hair dangled out of place. She had barely touched dinner, having drunk three "medicinal" teas instead.

Dad gently smoothed the stubborn pieces of hair back into place.

"You have to learn to ignore her," he said.

"I can't, Harold. Just today I heard Ida saying you should have married a country girl."

"Since when have I listened to Ida?"

"Maybe a country girl wouldn't have lost your sons." Mom leaned on Dad's shoulder, her tears streaking his grey shirt.

"We could always try..." He stopped, his words hanging in the hot August air.

"You know I can't!" Mom pushed away from him, and ran out of the room. Dad shook his head and slowly followed.

I pressed my ear to the screen to hear them. A dog barking down the road filled the silence. Then Mom's voice screamed, "Francine Pearle Taylor! Come in here right now!"

"What do you think you're doing?" Dad asked.

"I'm going to fix this once and for all."

I ran into the living room, letting the screen door slam. I had learned by the time I was nine that it was better to come immediately when Mom called. But this time I wished I'd stayed outside.

Her steel grey eyes narrowed when she saw me. I caught a glint from the scissors in her hand, and froze.

"Bonnie, don't!" Dad's shaky voice warned.

Mom grabbed me by the ponytail. She was breathing hard. I felt the heat through her dress, and the cold blades against my neck.

"What did I do now?" I asked.

"You survived, Frannie," she whispered. She ripped the blades through my hair, the sharp tips grazing my ears as she snipped. I held my breath and thought, "God, let her hands be steady."

"Stop it, Bonnie!"

"No!"

She leapt upstairs, waving my ponytail in the air like a trophy.

"You want a son?" she yelled.

Dad and I ran upstairs, Dad taking them two at a time. Mom was sitting on the floor in my room, shredding my dresses into little pieces and flinging them into the hall.

"There!"

She gathered a few tattered remnants into her hand, then jumped on my bed and started dancing a hula, my hair in one hand, dress scraps in the other.

"Tomorrow I'll order you the best fishing rod I can find. Lord knows I can't buy a decent one at the general store in Madison."

"Bonnie, that's enough!" Dad recovered his voice.

"Look! We had us a boy the whole time." She laughed, her hips swaying under her lilac print dress. "We'll just tell everyone we made a mistake."

She slumped onto the mattress and stared dreamily at my face. "You even look better as a boy." She tousled my hair and asked, "What should we call him? How about Frank, after my daddy?"

"Whatever you want," Dad said, carefully lifting her into his arms and carrying her into their bedroom.

"Honey, isn't it wonderful? Maybe tomorrow you can teach Frank how to drive the tractor?"

"Maybe. Now get some rest."

I hung in the hallway like a shadow, picking up pieces of cotton and eyelet lace while Dad called Doc Wilson.

Doc brought his wife, as usual. Mrs. Wilson tried to fix my hair, but it was so bad, she had to cut almost all of it off. I looked like Aunt Ida's son when he had gone off to war. Just his hair didn't stick up like mine.

"It'll grow back," she promised and hugged me. I snuggled into her heavy arms, and wished she wouldn't let go.

* * *

Doc Wilson had told Mom to stay in bed, but she didn't listen. She was hosting the Social Club meeting the next day and was up at sunrise making pastries and delicate finger sandwiches. By the time I had crept into the kitchen she had already unwrapped the porcelain tea set with the bright pink roses and gold trim.

I sat at the table watching her nimble fingers cut the crust off thick pieces of bread.

"Frank, how long have you been up?" She smiled and handed me a finger sandwich. I sniffed it suspiciously. "Oh, just eat it, I know you'll like it." She arranged the sandwiches on a plate. "Your dad's out back working on the tractor, if you want to help him."

I stopped picking apart my sandwich. "Don't you want me to serve?"

"No, sweetie. Tea socials are no place for little boys. Now go outside before my guests arrive."

I gulped down the sandwich and bolted before Mom changed her mind. I hated sitting there, week after week, listening to those old biddies gossip about everyone while they stuffed their faces. It was just as well, I only had two pairs of ragged overalls to wear anyway.

Dad was leaning over the tractor engine, his arms and face blotched with grease. "You okay, Sunshine?"

My eyes started stinging, and I climbed over the engine for a hug.

"It'll be fine. She doesn't mean to do it." He set me down.

"I know, I just want her to get better." I traced my hands in the thick, dusty layer of dirt. "And I wish Auntie Ida would stop saying all those things."

"She doesn't mean any harm." Dad rubbed his grimy hands on his pants. "Why aren't you inside with the ladies?"

"Mom says boys don't drink tea," I reminded him.

Dad scowled. He slammed the engine cover closed. "How about getting some shoes on? Then we'll go for a ride."

"Okay!"

I skipped into the kitchen and saw Mom boiling some water. I made sure I was extra quiet, and gently closed the screen. As I snuck by the living room, I heard Aunt Ida whispering.

"Mrs. Wilson said she chopped off all her hair!" She paused, savoring the attention. "And now she's calling her Frank!"

"What should we do?" someone else whispered.

"Pretend it's normal." Aunt Ida burst into laughter.

Mom glided in like a swallow, and perched herself on the couch. "What did I miss?"

"Nothing, dear," said Aunt Ida.

My whole body trembled, and my little hands curled into tight fists. I stomped into the living room, until I was facing Aunt Ida.

She paled when she saw me, her pink rouge sticking out like two welts on her cheeks.

"It's all your fault," I blurted out. "If it wasn't for your big mouth, I'd still be a girl."

Aunt Ida took a sip of tea, glaring at me over the rim of her cup. "Bonnie, are you just going to sit there and let this child sass me?"

From the corner of my eye, I saw Mom shiver. Her saucer slipped to the floor and split into two perfect halves.

"You're not a boy," Ida growled, "so don't pretend like you are."

I looked behind her, and saw Dad watching from the kitchen.

"Who made you so perfect that you could talk bad about everyone else?" I demanded.

One of the ladies snickered, and tried to cover it with a cough. Aunt Ida's eyes darted around the room. All of the ladies started excusing themselves, and hovered by the door. Aunt Ida set down her cup, and shrunk away to join the others.

I waited for the door to close, then picked up the saucer. Mom's eyes were fixed on the broken porcelain.

"I'm sorry," she whispered.

"Dad will fix it," I said solemnly. I carried the broken saucer into the kitchen.

Dad was waiting, and when he saw me, swept me into his arms and spun me around until I was dizzy.

"That was the bravest thing I've ever seen," he said.

And for the first time in a long time, he laughed.

Dead Scenes by Lydia Nowak

when you tell me your story
I am reminded
of the first time
I saw death

Uncle Joe, two days after surgery,
lying in the brushed silver casket
curls of white satin
a halo about his head.
when no one was looking
I touched his hand,
pressed to his chest,
sure it would collapse
empty from donations to science,
from a failed heart

but that has little to do
with your uncle.
stumbling dazed up the two flat,
grasping the splintered wood railing
moist red knife slits
fading to fry streaks
painting his collar.
the dumb look on his face
placed by a bat to his head

you said he was trying
to stop a fight
between two ladies.
I asked if anyone called the police.
your fresh-licked brown eyes
looked away,
all eight years of you shrugged
distantly saying
no one came

your words, like Uncle Joe's chest
your eyes, his carefully folded
cold steel hands.
in my dreams
I see satin swirls
closing over
his starched painted face
and wake to wonder
what your night holds

Dichotomy by Joan Shea O'Neal

I stare out my window.
the horizon is filled with corn plants
valiantly attempting to fulfill
their promise to feed the nation.
nearby, a herd of cows huddles
under the lone oak tree, waiting for
the signal to begin their leisurely march back to the barn.

And I dream of mountains.

I check the thermometer.
it is ninety degrees and the sun has barely risen.
like the scorched earth, I long
for the staccato kisses of a summer shower
and the gentle caress of a cooling breeze.

And I dream of mountain air.

Not the dense, humid medium
with which I am familiar,
but a gaseous mix that is
Alien,
Invigorating,
Intoxicating
to these lungs accustomed
to processing the almost palpable
Midwestern ether.

I long
to hear the roar of falling water,
incessantly
mocking the puniness of man,
see the fragile beauty of
columbines,
make love
in a room where
the only extraneous heat
is the heat of passion.

Instead,
I live in the Midwest,
and I sweat and complain and
wonder why I choose to live in
a place that is only comfortable
for a fraction of the year.
but I know,
as did my ancestors,
why we do not leave.

Mountain soil can not support our roots.

Prairie Hearts

Because This Did Not Happen to Me
by Ann Oomen

My farmer friend, driving the black Ford loaded with grain
into town, saw ahead the quick swerve, squeal and sudden jerk,
      heard
the short deadly crunch and knew for a thing so fast, so hard
not much could be said. He pulled over anyway, blinkers flashing
on the frosted grass, ran to it, and through the shattered window
he could reach her hands and touch her face and so he did.
They never spoke he said, but talked with eyes over sirens
and with small, almost imperceptible squeezes of the hands.

And when I asked him what it was like, it took him weeks to tell
until finally, late over cheap wine his face changed
as if he'd found some small thing he'd looked for – there it was –
he said with calm, "Death came like a small seed..."
opened his thumb and forefinger slowly, and I took it
to mean when the husk opens in earth, but having never seen
how seeds or lives come apart, I was still afraid.

No Heartland Here by Nancy Peiffer

The heartland I know
has no Rockwell families
It's the home of hidden bruises
          and untold stories
Every photo album contains
                    tarnished memories
Strawberry-Rhubarb pie eaten amongst
          simmering secrets
Picture-perfect fields of corn
temporarily hide
          festering boils
             suffocated dreams
          and suspicious scars
A Thanksgiving together with smiling grandparents
          masquerades the madness
             sustains the illusions
          and invalidates collective anger

There are no sacred images
and America
                    has no heartland

At the Chicago Art Institute:
Matisse's *Bathers by a River* by Mary Damon Peltier

the tenderness of bellies

vulnerable navel

the flesh hand curves to touch

hip that rises   comes forward

silver-lit bone

stillness of motion

endlessly repeated

the river

the river

I-57
by Laura Smith Porter

They left Champaign on a curve of highway, curling past the stoplight just behind Eisner's Foods at the Country Fair Shopping Plaza, where refrigerator trucks sat propped up against the loading docks and men in parkas hurried to unload boxes. The road straightened just past the ramp and cut a flat, unwavering ribbon through the winter fields. Virginia aimed the Buick under the green metal sign pointing to 57 North, to Chicago, the white letters almost obscured in the spitting squall of this grey January afternoon. She passed the ugly salmon-colored buildings of the new junior college, closed now for the Christmas hiatus, and then suddenly they were in the country.

*   *   *

No matter how many hundreds of times she and Bud had made this trip, Virginia was always surprised by how quickly they left town behind them. It had taken forever to leave London when she was a child, travelling to her grandmother in Oxford. The train had crawled out of Victoria Station, idling past miles of grim warehouses and factories before at last the green fields appeared and she could eat the buttered bread her mother had packed.

But that was almost sixty years ago, and these Illinois fields were brown, scored by frozen ruts that fanned out across the prairie. Every few miles, a shadowed clump of farm buildings rose up out of the starkness. White houses, with blank, forbidding windows, squatted next to weathered red barns; the triangular spokes of windmills spun erratically in the wind, ticking time in slow, irregular half-turns.

Virginia glanced over at Bud, wedged as close to the door as his seatbelt would allow, his head buried in the pillow she had propped against the window. He was breathing through his mouth, and the rasping filled the car. This afternoon he had pulled himself off the couch immediately when she told him gently that it was time to leave, and almost eagerly slipped his arms into the heavy overcoat she held. At the hospital, the nurses would start a morphine drip and he would be more comfortable. They couldn't control the pain at home anymore.

*   *   *

Last summer, during the rounds of chemotherapy, Virginia and Bud had tried to make an adventure of the drive up, stopping to eat somewhere off the highway, going downtown to Marshall Fields before they had to check in at the hospital. It was a way to have a little normal time before the drugs took Bud away.

Hermits with thick caramel frosting; fat round scones crusty with sugar; frosted chocolate cookies like miniature cakes: they stood at the seventh floor bakery counter like children spending their allowance, determinedly self-indulgent. Sometimes Bud insisted that Virginia have a new dress; he sat on a pink and gold upholstered chair outside the fitting room in the 28 Shop while she paraded in front of the mirrors. Every week, they had lunch at a different restaurant – the Drake, Le Perroquet. The really good places they had always meant to try. They held hands across the table and talked, enjoying the unexpected ceremony of a glass of wine in the middle of the day.

Until suddenly there had been no more respite.

"Well, we've had a good run for our money now, haven't we, Ginny?" Bud had turned to her after the last chemo treatment and smiled.

Pearl Harbor Day, six weeks ago. An appropriate date for a former GI and his war bride, Virginia had thought. Dr. Das Gupta had sat on the edge of Bud's bed at Presbyterian St. Luke's and spoken softly, watching them with warm brown eyes. He was without his "team," a piece of medical jargon Virginia had rather liked at first, welcoming the image of experts on their side against a vicious opponent.

But now they had lost the game. The team captain had come alone to tell them that the cancer had spread into the liver.

Virginia had shuddered at Bud's coolness, but she was just as surprised at her own relief to be face-to-face with the truth, at last.

* * *

In the distance, a stand of poplars appeared, a natural windbreak against the inexorable roll of cloud and sky. As it grew closer, the graceful, pear-shaped trees separated into perfectly aligned individual flames.

Virginia accelerated until the speedometer read 65, and pushed in the cruise control. She was hungry, but she wanted to break the back of this trip before the weather got any worse. Usually they stopped in Kankakee to eat, about two-thirds of the way up. They took the middle exit and argued about whether to go to the coffee shop at the bottom of the ramp or to Howard Johnson's, through the light and to the left. Bud always wanted to go to HoJo's for chocolate chip ice cream. These days, she indulged him, though he rarely ate more than a few spoonfuls. It was another sign that things had slipped away from them.

She checked him again. Still sleeping, lulled by the sound of the spinning tires and the hum of the car's heater, cranked up on high. She'd drive on past Kankakee and they could stop at the truck stop in Peotone. They served wonderful ham and beans, thick and steamy in shallow white bowls, slopping over onto the formica table. Maybe that would just hit the spot.

She ached, an almost physical pain below her breastbone, for that ordinary place: the loud voices of truckers, throwing open the jangling door and stamping the snow off their boots as they called out to their friends; white mints and wrapped toothpicks in the same divided plastic container next to the cash register; waitresses who kept the weak coffee flowing all day long. If anybody had problems, death or divorce or sickness, at least they didn't tell you about them.

What was she going to do when he died?

Virginia rubbed her temples to push the thought away, just as she had all the other times.

What would she do?

It wouldn't be long now. Weeks, maybe days. The spectre of his actual death, the final words yet to be said, hovered at the edge of her consciousness. She had buried her parents; she knew those moments waited for her, lurking just out of sight; once they happened she would carry them with her for the rest of her life.

She permitted herself to feel the silence of the empty house. She saw their bedroom, cleared of medical paraphernalia; opened the closet door to find only her dresses and blouses; heard the country music that Bud loathed and that was Virginia's secret vice, blaring from the stereo in the front hall. She watched herself dance, shades drawn against the curiosity of neighbors. And a tremor of anticipation – dreadful, but somehow not altogether unpleasant – rippled inside her.

What would it be like to be alone, for the first time in nearly fifty years?

She had widowed friends. They babysat for grandchildren, and took a lot of classes. They constantly talked about the need to keep "busy," something that had always struck Virginia as pathetic: grown women, all of them healthy, without sense enough to pick up a book! Nor had she the slightest desire to show up on Andrea's doorstep like some overaged nanny and beg to take care of her grandsons, much as she loved them.

Maybe she should go back to England.

She could go home.

A wave of images washed over her, so evocative that she clenched the steering wheel in sudden, fierce excitement. The marquees of the theater district, double decker buses, the green expanse of Hyde Park, pigeons on the wide sidewalks. She imagined herself sitting at a small table at Fortnum and Mason's, reading and drinking a strong cup of tea. The barren rural countryside outside the car window disappeared completely, eclipsed by the noise and grime of London.

It had been so long since she had thought of England as home. Her sister Alice still lived in Kensington; she could find a flat nearby, start over again. Andrea could bring the boys to see her, she would pay their airfares; she'd have money. And she'd come back to the States, of course, to visit her friends and to tend Bud's grave –

Bud. She reached over to pull his hand into her lap. That long road still spun itself out ahead, hiding those final moments around the next curve, or maybe the next. The ache in her chest returned, stronger than before.

She drove under a viaduct and the sign for Monee loomed up ahead. They were only thirty miles from Chicago now. Deep in thought, she had sailed right past the Peotone exit.

Now the traffic picked up, and the overpass signs began to tick off the numbered streets. In the early dusk, the skyline that Bud loved to watch for was barely visible over the crest of the highway.

He still hadn't waked when she pulled off 57 onto the Ryan. She held his hand to her cheek, pressing the warm, thin fingers to her lips. Tears streamed down her face, tears of grief, and of exultation. What a terrible thing it was, the instinct to survive.

Chicago Winter, 1932
by Rita Reinert

The kids on Sarah's block checked the sky every day on their way home from school. That day in early December, it looked heavy and grey, like an old blanket – promising the first snowfall of the season.

Snow began to fall at sunset and kept a steady pace through dinner. On this windless night all was bright and clear. The snow fell in large flakes fluffy against the glow of the street lights. They glistened like wet lace so Sarah knew that it was great for packing. Together the snow, the lighted streets and the round silver moon gave the scene a sense of mid-day and domed the evening in unusual quiet.

Sarah fidgeted throughout dinner, eager to check the snowfall every five minutes, impatient to pull back the freshly hung parlor curtains.

This was her chance, now that she was 12 and in the seventh grade – her first opportunity to join the bigger kids who shovelled snow with their fathers as a proud mark of near-adulthood. Tonight was the night. She had to make her parents understand she wasn't their little girl any more. She had to be allowed out right after supper, to shovel snow and finally take her place with those who prided themselves on clearing the steps and sidewalks like adults.

She hurried through supper, the snow beckoning her. Her dad's gaze rested on her expectantly.

"Please, Dad, please," she said, hoping she looked as ready as she felt.

He gave her a long quizzical look, grinned and said, "O.K. get your boots and shovel."

Next door, Ed was shoveling his porch. He went to her school, but was in eighth grade. She tried to catch his eye, not simply to have him notice her as she usually did, but seeking acknowledgement of her new status. He smiled briefly, but turned back to the serious adult business of clearing snow from the front porch, shoveling his way down the steps and across the front walk.

The younger and still younger kids came out soon after – but not to shovel, just to play in the snow like the little kids they were.

The big kids finished clearing the snow, and quickly started the real business of the evening – snowball fights. Soon the bright, cold air was filled with flying ammunition from one end of the block to the other.

What a kaleidoscope of color. Mufflers, caps, gloves in reds, yellows, blues and greens threaded through darker shades of coats and jackets. All smelling of wet wool!

Sarah felt she'd been let loose, scooping up double hands full of snow cupped between mittens and formed into snowballs. I was right, thought Sarah, this is great for packing.

The snowballs kept coming. It was a free-for-all with dads laughing and calling to each other, falling down on the icy pavements and scrambling up again.

Soon the little ones were wet, cold and crying. Sarah saw mothers come out with only sweaters or shawls thrown over their shoulders to snatch the smallest children out of harm's way and into warm houses.

Sarah's father went inside. One by one, the other dads gave up too, leaving the field to seventh and eight graders and high school kids.

By then, Sarah and the others were engulfed in a white wonderland. All their familiar landmarks had smoothed themselves out into unrecognizable snowy sculptures. She had trouble finding Jennie in the group of kids who looked like snowmen, but in fact, that's what they had started to make. The base grew until somehow they forgot about a snowman and decided to make the largest snowball the world had ever seen.

Five or six kids pushed it down the sidewalk, eventually rolling it to the deserted street, where the snow was smooth, deep and unmarked by traffic. They rolled the snowball from fifty-fifth street to fifty-fourth street, back to fifty-fifth and all the way back again to fifty-fourth. It got harder to move as it grew. More kids joined in, and finally, there were sixteen pairs of hands and sixteen strong shoulders on this "detail," but a snowball of tightly packed wet snow ten feet in diameter was more then they could budge.

So they left it, smack in the middle of the intersection at fifty-fourth and Justine – to the amazement of the neighbors as they opened their doors the next morning.

That morning was full of surprises. They had no school that day! But there was more – the City of Chicago called this "Great Snowball" a traffic hazard and sent four men and two trucks from the Department of Streets and Sanitation to demolish it. Sarah and her friends begged them to let it be, but they just looked mad. If it hadn't been for these kids, they wouldn't have to be out on this cold, blustery day.

When the city workers asked the kids who was responsible for this foolishness, the answers were "Nada," "Ich spreche kein Englisch," and "Nie mowie po Angielsku." Suddenly, no kid on the block could speak English. One of the truck drivers stared at Sarah. She recognized him as a friend of her father and quickly scooted to the back of the pack. He knew she spoke perfect English.

The city workers swore and sweated in the cold during the long time it took them to break it up with picks and shovels. Finally, they pushed the frozen core to the curb.

The "Great Snowball" became legend, and with it, Sarah and the kids who started the whole thing. On the next snowy evening, five days later, men in fedoras and top coats swarmed all over Sarah's quiet block. Her father said they were city workers making sure that it would not happen again.

* * *

Later that winter, Sarah and Jennie came to appreciate Chicago's snow clearing crews when they plowed 54th Street, leading the way to Sherman Park where the shallow lagoon was frozen over. The annual wait to skate had begun.

Since she was now one of that select group who was allowed to skate at night, Sarah waited through three cold days in a row for the ice to be ready for testing. She first heard it would happen from Jennie, her best friend, who heard it from Danny, who knew from his older brothers who hung around the cops in the park. That's how the word was spread, so that afternoon, kids from three different schools; St. Augustine, St. John of God and Arthur A. Libby raced to the park to witness this annual winter phenomenon.

Two policemen walked behind a couple of reined horses, all across the solid surface of the lagoon. That was the test – it determined that the ice was thick enough for skating. A great cheer went up when the team reached safety. They never broke through, not that year nor any before or after.

Although the lagoon spanned three square blocks around "the island," it was only three feet deep. Once frozen, the ice was good until March. Then the "Danger" signs went up again.

City workmen had already set up the "Hot House," a long, low, frame building trucked in each year. Inside, it was partitioned, boy's side/girls' side.

Each side had a large pot–bellied stove which Mac, the cop, kept fed with logs all evening. There were a couple of bare light bulbs hanging from electrical cords in both sections. If they got broken, which happened sometimes on the boys' side, they were in the dark for the rest of the evening. That made it harder for the boys to find their shoes when they took their skates off, but Jennie and Sarah heard that most boys had a secret place in the rafters to hide their shoes, so light didn't make a lot of difference to them. The lights on the girl's side never got broken.

Sarah loved the rustic old "Hot House" with all those initials and dates and hearts carved in the two-by-fours. It was somehow much more than just a place to put on her skates. She came in to warm her hands and feet at the fire and later still, while Mac was hurrying everyone out so he could lock up for the night, she met boys from other schools, older boys from other grades and other blocks – boys who waited outside in the cold for the girls, like Ed. She would never have met them except for these special occasions of freedom, to be allowed out on wintery nights to try out new Christmas skates.

Sarah and her friends glowed with rosy cheeks, bright eyes and with shiny strands of wet hair peeking out from under woolen caps as they walked home along fifty-fourth street in the light of the bright January moon.

"This is almost like daylight," Ed said behind her, "but eerie."

She turned, startled, as he reached for her skates and slung them over his shoulder. Could this be happening?

The cold night air hurried them. Sarah saw her breath in front of her as she talked, only half aware of what she was saying, and not at all aware of the others, she was so overwhelmed at being with

Ed, the first boy she'd liked who was actually walking her home on her first winter as an almost-adult.

"Look at all those stars in the sky," he said.

"Perfect for the first night of skating," she said. And the first night of my new life, she thought.

Tornado
by Mie Hae Rhee

"Injoo, did you bring in the hot peppers for *gihmchee* from the back yard?" Sooja asks.

"No, mom, it's only 5:30, and the sun is still hot. They'll dry well if we leave them for a little longer," Injoo answers as she prepares supper.

"You never listen to me. Will you ever obey your mother? I told you whenever I feel the arthritis in my fingers, I know it will rain any minute." Injoo feels the irritation in her mother's voice, signaling a meaningless fight.

"Why don't you ask your favorite granddaughter, Kathy? She's done with her homework and is playing with her dolls in the family room. You tamed her like a dog to obey you." Injoo can be sarcastic.

"Forget it," Sooja says. "It was my mistake asking you. I've told myself a million times that I wouldn't ask you to do anything, but I keep forgetting. I'll do it myself."

Sooja goes through the utility room to reach the back door and finds their dog, Badoogee, scratching at the door to go out. When Badoogee sees Sooja, he barks and leaps on her leg. Sooja picks Badoogee up. He is trembling and pushes his head under Sooja's arm.

"What's the matter with you?" Sooja pushes the door to go out, and the dog whines in her arms. Finally, she puts him down and he runs out like lightening.

"Something must be wrong." Sooja looks outside. The sun is shining, but dark clouds are moving in quickly. Sooja loves to look at the wild Midwest prairie behind their backyard. She admires the beauty of the spacious fields, and wonders how it was formed without any mountains and brooks. She especially enjoys watching the splendid sunset which reminds her of the peaceful farm village in Korea where she grew up. But the black clouds in the middle of the prairie move in so fast she can only see some trees.

Looks like a storm, she thinks, I'd better bring in the red peppers before the rain starts.

Out of nowhere, Sooja hears an eerie loud whistle sound followed by a great thundering sound and sees a whirling mass of dust coming toward the house. Frightened, she grabs the shaking door knob. Suddenly, she feels herself sucked up into the sky and hears faint screams from inside the house.

* * *

Minutes later when Sooja opens her eyes, the first thing she sees is the black sky.

Where am I? She wonders. How long have I been here? She is covered with torn and fallen lumber, tree branches, and other debris. Dazed, she realizes that she is lying on the ground. Looking up, she sees that some of the big trees in her backyard have snapped in half. Moving her head, she sees the storm has thrown all kinds of furniture, clothes, toys, tin cans and newspapers into her backyard.

She tries to pull herself up and realizes she is wet. The grass beneath her is wet, too.

She feels a dull pain in her right leg and rolls to the side, pushing against the ground to sit up.

Checking her leg, she finds bruises next to the varicose veins and scars from ancient wounds, but no blood.

"Woof, Woof"

"Badoogee!" The dog's bark brings back Sooja's memory. She remembers the red pepper, Badoogee, and the shaking door knob, thoughts that make her shiver.

Remembering those faint screams from the house, she worries. What happened to Injoo? Turning her head, she sees her home. "I can't believe my eyes," she says to the wreckage around her. She can see the back door has been broken down, and the utility room through the doorway. The washer and dryer are smashed, the shelves and cabinets ripped off the wall. Everything is scattered all over the floor. She hears Badoogee's bark coming from the far end of the house.

Sooja limps to the front side of the house feeling that it takes her forever. Finally, she gets to the front, stops and cries. "All the windows are shattered. Part of the roof has collapsed. I don't even know where the front door was.

"My daughter! She was in the kitchen when this happened."

Forgetting the pain in her leg, Sooja drags herself to the back door. She tries to clear all the fallen shelves and debris from the doorway but is too short to reach the top of the pile. She finds a bucket blown in from nowhere, puts it upside down and stands on top of it. Continuing to pull things down, she feels sharp edged pieces of wood and rusty nails that have broken off the cabinets and shelves. The washer and dryer still block the doorway, and she has to climb over the machines.

Sooja cries out, "Injoo, my poor daughter! Are you there? Are you okay? Injoo, your mom is coming, I love you. I promise never to scold or criticize you again." She takes a deep breath. "It's getting dark. I'd better hurry."

She can't see well because of tears. She gropes her way in the dark, squats, start to crawl. The inside of the house is now even darker than outside.

"Injoo, can you hear me? When I learned your father was missing in the Vietnam War, you were only two years old. I lived only for you. If I didn't have you, I would have died." Sooja coughs because of the dust. "I was so strict with you when you were growing up because you were my only child and I didn't want you to be spoiled." Sooja remembers how hard it had been raising a child without a father. When Injoo was a toddler, she asked Sooja to buy a father. She thought I could buy a father like a doll. When Injoo was in kindergarten, she begged Sooja to be married so she could have a father.

"I kept hoping your father would return home some day. I wanted to show him his beautiful daughter who had grown to be such a fine lady. That was my dream." Sooja murmurs.

"Do you hear me, Injoo? Answer me! I'm so sorry I was against your marriage to Hohmin. I thought Hohmin was not as good as you were. I am so sorry, I said the heavens punished you when Hohmin was killed in that automobile accident."

The house is so dark, I can't see anything, Sooja thinks as she crawls over shattered window panes, shredding her hands and knees. The fear that she might not be able to save her daughter makes her almost crazy. Her hands are becoming red pulp. Still, she continues, ignoring the pain and blood. Her mind is fixed only on saving her daughter. She is sixty years old, and her daughter, born after three miscarriages, is twenty-nine. I know I've been over protective, and I know you resented it. Sobbing, Sooja clears a path inch by inch deep inside the house.

She scrapes her left arm on the broken utility room sink. Feeling her flesh tear, Sooja screams, hearing her voice echo for long moments through the house. Can it be they are all dead?

Finally, Kathy calls, "Grandma, Grandma!"

"Woof, Woof!" The dog barks after Kathy.

"Where are you, Kathy?" Sooja calls. "Where is your mother?"

"I don't know. I'm scared. Help me, just help me get out. Grandma!"

Injoo is dead, Sooja fears. "Injoo, you cannot die before me. You have to be okay. Oh, God! Help her, please."

Sooja hears Kathy call again and Badoogee barks without stopping.

"Oh, Grandma, can't you come help me? It hurts. Owww."

"Wait Kathy. Grandma is coming." Sooja thinks, If only I could see . . . Moving in the direction of Kathy's voice, she hears a moaning sound. She stops, and listens. The sound is very weak. If Injoo were not her daughter, she might not even recognize it as Injoo's voice. "Are you there? Injoo?" She turns her body to the opposite direction and moves much faster. Obstacles are no longer problems to her.

Kathy calls out to her again.

"Grandma, Grandma, The bookshelves fell on me. I can't move!" Sooja ignores Kathy and keeps moving toward Injoo's moans. Badoogee jumps at Sooja's skirt. But she moves still faster. Feeling something with her hands, she shouts.

"Injoo! Is it you, Injoo?" This time she touches Injoo's head and face. "I'm so glad that you're alive! Are you okay?"

Before Injoo replies, Badoogee barks softly, "Woof." The dog has been watching over Injoo. Sooja now understands why Badoogee was so scared and ran away. She realizes animals have special instincts to detect a natural calamity. Yet, he is faithful and has returned to stay at Injoo's side.

"Injoo, are you all right?" Sooja asks again.

"Mom, I'm okay," Injoo answers in a small voice. "Go help Kathy."

Sooja lifts the broken chair pieces from her daughter, sweeping aside pieces of glass that cut her hands.

In the meantime, Kathy's screams sound even more desperate.

"Mom," Injoo says, "please go and help Kathy. If anything happens to her, I can't live."

"Well, if anything happens to *you*, I can't live, Injoo."

Sooja is surprised at her own words. She really thought she loved Kathy more than Injoo. Ever since Injoo married against Sooja's will, she told everybody that she didn't love Injoo anymore. She acted like she didn't care if anything happened to Injoo and thought that she was living for her granddaughter, Kathy.

She turns, moving toward the sound of Kathy's wails, marveling to herself, it took a tornado to make me realize how much I love my daughter.

American Still Life by Kim Rinn

The nicotine stained clock
signals the vast evening swell;
diners in peanut butter colored shoes
bury worn faces in menus
as familiar as Wednesday's ham on rye.
Their bald heads moon waitresses
dressed in the color of spun candy
hovering like angels around Jesus.
Promises of mansions and satellite dishes
are buried here under crumpled lotto tickets.
No shooting stars for granting wishes.
No parting rivers to speed escape.
Nothing to prevent the scene repeating
until the neon OPEN flashes off.

Celebrating the West by Marcia Schwartz

Ancient shadows floated over the dancing water,
As the vacant thunder lit up the big sky.
Captured Pony went in search of the blue swallows,
While the floating rivers swiftly drifted by.

The pride of the warrior shared a vision with the dream weaver,
For through the eyes of an eagle he saw the sacred connection.
Hidden treasure was said to be buried in the beaver pond,
And the Trading Post stood as its sole protection.

Horses, mules and men came down from the high country,
While the smoke messenger rose high towards the sky.
As the approaching storm darkened the Black Mesa,
The gentle rain fell and the wagon train passed by.

The bold eagle soared down over the mountain
As Swift Runner chased the buffalo down to the stream.

Ghosts of countless memories are on the march again,
While the Cowboys and Indians both pursue their dreams.

Hot September
by Whitney Scott

Years ago, I heard Jimmy got busted for dealing — crack cocaine to teens and pregnant women, the media reported. And because he was a repeat user with a rap sheet, the judge didn't diddle around with suspended sentences or treatment programs or community service, or any of that hoopla anymore — just sentenced him to seven to fifteen in the pen, eligible to walk in three. They held him for a while at the charm school at 26th and California, then shipped him out, out, out.

I'm not the one to bring it up when I run into him — at the Art Institute, of all places! Jimmy the jock whose artistic preferences ran to sports posters and pin-ups, no doubt, if I'd even known him well enough to see the inside of his house.

Not that it would have happened — seeing each other outside of high school, I mean, because I was the socially conscious class poet, kind of beatnik-y in those days early in the '60s, with the black stockings, white lipstick and all, full of the smug self-righteousness that came from being one of few in my community who'd heard of passive resistance, Allen Ginsberg and bongo drums. He, on the other hand, yearned to play professional basketball. So we didn't exactly run in the same circles. In fact, I deplored the institutionalized privilege he symbolized, this "shooting star" destined for swift and lasting fame — with his retinue of hero-worshippers, his powerful, loping walk, his push-ups and sweat, his growing renown for nearly legendary speed and agility.

Jimmy typified the mentality then of that dusty, one-road town 90 minutes south of Carbondale, Illinois, which seemed an unreachable physical, emotional and cultural distance from the promise of

Chicago. He was openly contemptuous of me and the few others in our group, distinguished by our brainy disdain for the football, basketball, track and baseball that defined the seasons of hope in our high school years and focused the attentions of our small town's smaller minds.

Actually, for people whose lives and goals were so different, Jimmy and I seemed to run into each other a lot at our tiny school in downstate Union County with its graduating class of only 23 students — chance encounters often punctuated by mutual insults of "illiterate" from me and "dog face" from him if any of our friends were around. Strangely, if we were alone when our paths crossed at school, he rarely spoke, just looked down at me intently, occasionally saying, "Hi," in a hoarse whisper while I remained mutely locked into the pain of his past mockeries.

Sometimes I glimpsed Jimmy huddled over our English text in a far corner of the town's largely disused library, caught him looking at me more than once, even thought I saw him coming over a couple of times, but he veered away from my table at the last minute, all pink in the face beneath his short blond hair. I found myself with a sense of sorrow for him as I saw his efforts in class to make sense of the stories and poems we read, almost feeling his struggle as he negotiated the minefield of clauses in a compound-complex sentence. But after watching him shrug off his academic inadequacies to his all-forgiving fans which included the majority of the school's teachers, I'd reclaim my disdain, wishing the worst for that self-assured, swaggering moron whose life force seemed directed toward sinking baskets.

Often I saw him as I walked home from my after-school study group in the early evening — Jimmy practicing foul shots and lay-ups alone, long after the rest of the team had gone to the showers. One hot September evening the heat still shimmered in the still air though the sun was dropping lower in the sky. He must have been drilling for hours, for he was soaked with sweat, his wet pullover thrown on the ground so that he stood shirtless, revealing wet, glistening mounds of muscle defining a broad back still red from summer sun, accentuating his small, round rear in green gym shorts. The slanting rays silhouetted him as he raced through blindingly intricate patterns of fancy footwork all over the court, one moment at the free-throw line, yet magically touching the hoop in an eye's blink, skimming the ground so fast he blurred in the fading light, his long, floppy shoelaces whipping like froth in all directions. He darted through the moves intently, shot after shot, beads of wetness whirling into the air as he bounded and soared with a dancer's graceful ecstasy, rivulets running a river down his chest, disappearing into the corrugated elastic of his waist band.

After an hour it grew too dark for him to continue. Still radiating energy, he picked up his wet shirt and walked away without ever seeing me watching from the deepening shadows.

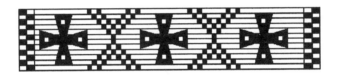

We left our homes near the Trail of Tears scenic route for out-of-state colleges, both via scholarships, but very different kinds. He leapt to the pros after just two years of school, a major rookie draft choice according to the news, and destined for the meteoric rise to stardom he'd dreamt of. My grades, fueled by all-night study sessions, took me to Oxford for my junior year so I lost touch with Jimmy's life for awhile. Though America was ripped by civil rights protests, flag burnings and street demonstrations then, the lure of the counter-culture was shifting for me to more practical career concerns, the world of jurisprudence. In a short time, Jimmy's swift rise in the NBA earned him a place as the New York Knicks' starting center, and I was sleeping only four hours a day and studying 15 to maintain my class standing at Fordham Law School.

Shortly after, the first stories of Jimmy's alleged drug use surfaced, followed by extensive media coverage of his arrests, suspensions, press conferences, treatment programs, two come-backs, and another series of arrests with well-publicized warnings and sentences of community service. By his third and last attempt to resuscitate his career, I was a rising young star, bright and shining in my work at a large Chicago firm specializing in corporate tax law for its large roster of Blue Chip clients. Occasional pro bono work for some of the Plains Indians organizations helped me feel politically correct.

Now here he is, out of jail and the NBA — sitting on the Art Institute steps, dressed in old sweats with the sleeves cut off and Converse hi-tops that are falling apart. Surprisingly, Jimmy recognizes me, calls my name, though it's been so many years since we've seen each other. He rises unsteadily, gazing at my briefcase, suit and heels, and when I tell him I'm an attorney, surprises me again by congratulating me, by saying he'd always known I'd go on to be somebody — his pale, thin face showing no hint of hypocrisy, just an inexplicable relief he seems to feel at this random encounter.

His hair is still mostly blond, but no longer boot-camp short and without its youthful jock vitality as it falls, lusterless, over his large-eyed face.

"I was in the pen at Stateville for a few years," he tells me haltingly, with the sad certainty that he expects me to know, and more, to care — God knows why. I say nothing and he continues, "That's all over now, and I'm not never going back."

I nod and he goes on, his pupils pinpricks in the overcast light of early evening, "I've learned a couple, three things and let me tell you, that part of my life's behind me. I'm a changed man on a new road..."

Tuning him out, I imagine him on the bleak downward cycle of repeat sentences that almost assuredly await him, foresee his early death from drugs and disease and hate Jimmy all over again, this time with an new purity of loathing that almost shakes me — hatred for his wasted body, talent and life, revulsion for the sweet possibilities and promises of his past and my own, when all things waited, open and inviting.

I wished him the worst all those years ago, and what's so funny is, it's happened. You'd think it would make me happy, or at least smug. But all I can think of as I turn and hurry down the steps is that beautiful, bare-chested boy framed in twilight that hot September evening, racing over the court, a lightning streak of sweat and fancy footwork in the dusk, moving so fast he's a blur.

True Confessions by Patty See

The summer Coke changed its recipe back
to Classic and Sally Jesse Raphael moved from radio
to TV, I sweltered over a grill in the screened Falls
Drive-In kitchen turning burgers and dropping fries
or I fitted trays to car windows, waiting for fifteen
to bump into sixteen and transform me from carhop

to sultry teen beauty. The Farrrah-haired carhops,
busty and tan, swiveled aprons and necks. Down my back
hung a kinky mop I'd hid behind for all of my fifteen
years. Most shifts I watched the highway, radios
blasting from cars driving past or I memorized a fried
food litany: pizza burger, pronto pup, ribette – all falling

into a chain – zebra cone, slop, polar bear. Chippewa Falls
girls were separated, hot items from cold. An older carhop
matter-of-factly told me, while dropping curds into the fryer,
You Catholic girls have it easy, no guilt, just pay-back
with Novenas. I shrugged, listening for some distant radio.
A week later we guzzled Andre pink bought for $2.15

a bottle and closed Babe's Bar where even fifteen
was old enough. After my first acknowledged fall
it got easier to feign experience, turn up the radio
with public school boys and their dollar tips. I carhopped
each week away and Fridays I ran to the bank and back,
or face to face confessed my sins, still afraid of frying

in hell. The worst I penanced myself, silently deep frying
away with half-chicken Sunday dinners. At fifteen
a Hail Mary for every boy or Glory Be for every beer backed
up my lies quick as a reorder slip. I spent slow days at the Falls
playing tic tac toe alone and learned from the other carhops
that most boys were really not the stuff that made radio

love songs, but a trick of x'es and oh's. I tuned the radio
with one hand, slid patties into buns or bagged fries
with the other, and became the only known carhop
who delivered a six-pak of cones in one trip. At fifteen
I carved my name into the red counter of the Falls
Drive-In, joining thirty years of names etched back

on June days playing the same greasy radio, girls
a breath past fifteen, frying in the same tiny kitchen,
knowing a boy has fallen when he sticks to you
like a tray to a window. And wondering
if – like carhops – only the start of an engine
or the honk of a horn can bring him back.

Carmen
by Jennifer Sheridan

My best friend Carmen leaned against the sink and arched her back. She blew smoke at the ceiling and it curled back down the face of the mirror behind her. She was telling me the story of her virginity in that slow, sultry way she had. She'd just finished the orgasm part. We were cutting all our Monday afternoon classes and sharing a cigarette in her dorm bathroom.

It had happened over Thanksgiving break the previous week, in Greece with an older cousin who spoke no English. Late, nearly dawn. Parted French doors. An ocean.

I draped my arms over the still warm hand dryer. Carmen's tan was a deep berry color that rolled out of the sleeves of her tee shirt.

"Afterwards he paced around the room," she whispered. I pictured a leopard crisscrossing by the open window. Outside the sky would glow lavender. A breeze. The sound of water. The smell of salt and sky and beach.

"What did it feel like?"

"Watching him pace?"

"Yeah." I pictured myself in her place, lying on starched white sheets as my first lover, foreign and chiseled, paced like a wild animal.

"It was awesome," she said. "It was my favorite part." Passing the cigarette, she gave me a smile no one else for miles ever saw. She knew the pacing part would be my favorite too.

"God, Carmen, leave it to you to have the perfect first time," I said.

"Let's get drunk," she suggested. I nodded, dropping the half-smoked cigarette into the sink. It landed in a fierce sizzle.

* * *

By five-thirty the pint of Jack Daniel's was finished and the dinner migration began. When Aaron Klinger sauntered by Carmen's doorway he winked at me. Aaron Klinger who'd phone me late at night. *What was I doing? Nothing much.* I'd follow the scent of stale cigarettes into his bed. But it was a secret.

I thought I might throw up after all the booze, and Aaron winking at me, so I dug another vanilla wafer out of the box and drank some tap water out of my cupped palm. Carmen lay face down on her bed, trying to light a cigarette.

At six-fifteen her date appeared, standing at the door for God knows how long before I noticed him. Byron. He had black pubic-curly hair on his face and head, and bugged-out eyes. His hands fluttered over his chest, landing at his sides.

Carmen insisted I come to an ancient Warren Beatty film that I'd seen twice to make sure I really hated, but what the hell, Carmen wanted me to go.

*   *   *

During the movie I watched her face flicker in the light coming off the screen. Occasionally I saw Byron glaring at me from the other side. I thought about Aaron, how we smoked in silence sometimes, afterward, staring at the ceiling, not touching.

"Kate," he once said. "You know Scott, the football player?"

"Yeah?"

"Well, every day he goes to this one girl's room and they do it." He leaned on one elbow and tapped his cigarette into the ashtray lying between us. I pulled the sheet up to my chin. "She makes him a cheese omelet, and that's it." Aaron rested his chin on my sheet-covered chest. His greasy hair fell onto the back of my hand as I stroked the nape of his neck.

"That's great, Aaron," I said.

*   *   *

In the science auditorium a ten-foot Warren Beatty leaned into an open refrigerator against a half-naked Goldie Hawn.

"Juicy bootie," Carmen growled. I laughed, but I felt a hundred years old. I just wanted to go home. Maybe the phone in my hallway would be ringing. Maybe my brother would call from Yale.

"Hey, Sis, how's that Anthro class?" He'd never called me from Yale. He didn't know what classes I had.

Outside the air smelled of frost. Carmen sang a Christmas carol. Byron jammed his hands into his pockets, his eyes on Carmen, twirling in and out of sight on perfect ballet points.

"My mother is such a bitch," she said. "I hate her guts." I thought about flannel sheets against my naked skin.

"She's just drunk," I mumbled to Byron.

"Kiss me," Carmen screamed, grabbing him. She knew how bad he wanted her. I thought it was cruel, the way she treated guys. But maybe I was wrong to feel bad. Byron didn't give a shit about her either. He wanted what he wanted, we all did. At the time I gave everyone a million times more credit than they deserved.

Byron puckered his skinny chapped lips. I could see them quiver in the moonlight. Carmen wouldn't be happy about this in the morning, if she remembered it at all.

"Carmen..." I started. Carmen was in my face like a guard dog.

"Mind you're own fucking business," she screamed.

"Yeah," said Byron. His hand gripped her arm. Carmen turned to him with a low laugh. I tried again. This time she whipped around and slapped me hard across the face. We all heard the sound. While I stroked the stinging place on my cheek his arm wrapped around her back, sliding down over her ass. She squeaked a little as he kissed her. Carmen pulled away, almost falling over backwards. Byron licked his lips and steadied her with his spindly hands.

"Good night to you," she slurred. She'd forgotten his name. Carmen disappeared into the darkness. When I found her she was throwing up in the bushes. I half-dragged her to her room.

Carmen pulled her limp dress over her head and fell naked onto the bed. She laughed at me, standing by the sink holding an empty vanilla wafer box. I could see her shape in the dim light from the hall.

"I do love you, Katie," she mumbled, rolling toward the wall. I hung her dress on the closet doorknob and stood very still on her carpet. She whimpered slightly, a sharp stab, then nothing.

I took the two steps to the side of the bed. She rolled onto her back, cradling her long arm behind her head.

"My mom," she said.

"I know," I whispered. I pulled the damp hair out of her eyes and smoothed it down along her pillow. She smelled terrible, of vomit and whiskey. She sobbed again. Her eyelids fluttered. I ran my hand over her forehead. She leaned into my fingers, cool against her hot skin. I kissed her cheek and pressed my face against hers.

Suddenly Carmen came to life. She wrapped her sweaty, strong arms around my neck and pulled my face to hers by my hair. I clamped my jaw shut, stifling a scream. Adrenaline shot through me so fast my fingers shot out straight. The next thing I knew her mouth was on mine, her lips grinding against me, her tongue forcing my teeth apart. Carmen, my best friend. Her mouth felt swollen and hot, but her tongue was cooler. It glided finally past my stubborn teeth, into my mouth. Only after she had fallen back onto the bed, eyes shut, breathing even and deep did I feel the sensation of our tongues together, like warm snakes in a twisting, sinewy pile.

When I stood up my legs wobbled. Carmen's naked chest rose and fell, half under the sheet. I staggered through the door and up the stuffy hall. One long, florescent lightbulb flickered purple as I passed under it.

* * *

In the morning Carmen called me on the phone.

"God, Katie," she laughed. "I feel like hell."

I was angry, not because she'd slapped me but just because of everything. She wore me out. I'd watched her dance and flirt and held her head while she barfed. Carmen wasn't meant for quiet, midwestern evenings. Her green-tinted skin and wild ways, her elegance made me hate myself.

She admitted sheepishly that she'd been pretty drunk the night before. No, she didn't remember the movie, or spilling her Raisinets, licking melted chocolate from her fingers.

"Do you remember kissing Byron?" I asked.

"I didn't."

"Do you remember slapping me?"

"Katie, I never did!"

"Yeah, you sure did."

I thought about Carmen putting badly typed love letters signed with Aaron's name in my mailbox, Carmen calling at two a.m. to talk about Ingmar Bergman, Carmen saying I looked like a Gypsy princess in the sweater I was sure people thought was weird.

"Katie, did I? Tell me I didn't."

"You didn't."

"I did, didn't I."

"Yeah, you did."

"I'm sorry, Katie," she said. "Do you forgive me?"

I forgave Carmen. I met her for lunch. She looked the same. Standing at the bottom of the stairs leading up to the dining hall her hands did not shake. She reached for me, a fake worried look on her face.

"Help me up the stairs, daughter," she said in an old lady voice. "I feel like shit." She leaned against me as we climbed the stairs, mumbling how much coffee she would need, twenty-nine cups, black.

We blew off all our classes that day. We smoked and laughed and bought a bottle of gin. Coming out of the liquor store Carmen said she'd call her evil, stingy father for more money.

"If I'm lucky my mom will answer the phone. She always throws in an extra fifty," she said.

Sitting in the grass outside the library Carmen apologized again and shook her head, smiling into her lap. I watched her bring her cigarette to her lips. I watched her close her eyes. I listened to the ache behind her laugh that only I ever heard. I told her a thousand times to forget the whole thing. I promised to forget it myself. I really had no choice in the matter.

Chicken Money by Joan Shroyer-Keno

She fed chickens
that laid eggs
she mixed with flour,
salt and water
and rolled thin and square
as pages in her Bible
that fed her soul.

Noodle-cakes were her
words for golden sheets
of dough she dried
in sunshine each weekday
on beds upstairs,
then rolled into scrolls,
and sliced with her knife.

"Full of Noodles"
said her handwriting
on brown paper bags
her son filled by the ounce,
thumb on scale,
when he sold them
at hi store on Saturday.

Her cleaver was quick
to kill chickens for
soup to feed preachers
who said grace on Sunday,
and took her tithe, too.

Assembly Line by Joan Shroyer-Keno

The white enamel tubs sat on our
porch on a cruel November
day. Uncle Ray's great belly
grunted when he hauled the first one

into our snug kitchen. He hefted
globs of red flesh above his head with
his big beefy hands and toasted
the next nine hours with his annual

question: "That's about a
pound, ain't it, Mom?" The thud of
Bessie-through-a-meat-grinder
met waxed paper. Aunt Loretta

shaped a square as she wrapped
then passed to Grandma for a
second packaging in heavy brown
paper. Cousin Sue cut the tape,

and I wrote: HAMBURGER, 1 LB,
BESSIE, 1968. Grandpa finally stacked
her in our long, deep, cold, white
Frigidaire freezer, pound by pound.

Samples by Kelly Sievers

Johanna Mulvihill McMahon
1850-1913

Johanna, let me walk along with you.
Crossing prairie fields to your township,
we can take the route you follow early June,
your book of samples balanced on your hip.
Slow your pace from house to house, I want to sit
at kitchen tables, watch you turn the pages
of taffetas, satins, cotton voiles and eyelets;
hear you praise your ginghams and chambrays.
Let's stay for tea, talk of family and wages.
Between plans for draperies and jumpers
for young daughters, tell us how you manage
Will, Jim, and Kate since you lost their father.
I see your book of samples shifts your gait.
Johanna, let me help you with its weight.

Secrets: Milwaukee, 1970 by Kelly Sievers

Decide. Call one clinic.
Call another. Roll your
sleeve for the nurse. Aim
for the cup. Say it,
"Please, I am afraid ..."
Listen: *No one*
will know. Copy the name.
Don't ask why he
must sign, climb the steps
to the minister. Answer
his questions; stare
at his desk, the soles of his shoes.
Write down the number. Find
a pay phone. Find enough
quarters. Listen: *One hundred*
dollars. Borrow from your
brother. Tell him your car
needs work. Charge
a round trip ticket. Go
alone. Go at night. They do
them on West Sixty-
ninth. Read the address
to the cab driver. Watch
the ash on his cigarette.
Watch the rain.
How many weeks?
Where is the father?
Swallow the pills. Slide
your skirt up; remove
pantyhose, underwear.
Here are the stirrups. Here
is the doctor's bald head. Now
you will bleed.

Prairie Hearts

The El Tunnel by Claudia Rosa Silva

I. I hear the sweet beat he plays
ringing in a foreign tunnel.
It echoes through me.
I walk briskly to his rhythms,
drawn by vibrant melodies
bright and hot in flourescent lights as I approach.
I try not to stare
but his eyes – vivid, black, hold mine,
playing for my notice.

II. He sings with passion
Words in African tongues unknown to me
with their bongo beat,
his dark hands pounding,
head bobbing
in its cap of green, yellow, red and black.
He sees within me my Latina pride
of green, white and red
and breaks his song,
breaks the wall between us –
singing, *"Mira, mira,"*
"look, look" as I pass through
his life,
his streams of song
immersing me.

III. The energy of his music
draws me to turn my head,
turn the corners of my mouth
to an unsure smile,
feeling special he sang to me.
The sweet beat he plays
links me to our song of life,
echoing through us.

Icy Drive to Lincoln State School for the Mentally Retarded* (January, 1973)
by Margie Skelly

Just out of Chicago, the ruthless rain
falls aimlessly on trees, sticks, bushes:
cold, colder, Coldest.

In Normal, open the car window just a creak.
Hear the ice crying, the murmur of something
that tried to be born but didn't make it.
Close the window now; protect yourself.

Mother Nature grips the foliage in her hands,
smothers the deaf dumb wood with frozen water,
clenching it like a parent.

Icy shield on the greens and browns of Bloomington,
the colorless mishaps by the side of the road,
things to peer at through frosty car windows.

Nature is all around you on Interstate 55:
Silver twisted forms, trees upside down,
some bending to the ground,
some uncertain of their direction.

Flashing-white-silver,
God took her sparkler and made a day of it:
Central Illinois has become Pluto.

You *are* on another planet,
a crippling shining uncertainty.
The silver screams at you.
Even the blades of grass are helpless needles
that can't mend the disaster.

Soon daylight dissolves into night light
and you can still see the silver climbing
into the sky like smoke from a cigarette that rises,
then falls.

Finally you arrive:
A seasonal guest at
Lincoln State School for the Mentally Retarded.
You want a night cap as you leave your car
by the light of the alien moon.

*Lincoln State School for the Mentally Retarded was in operation in the early 1970's.

The Road to Recovery
by Grazina Smith

I lay in the hospital bed, hemorrhaging, while the Rosenbergs died. Waking this morning, I find a dusting of red and black pepper specks on my sheet. I had not eaten anything the previous day, so I'm surprised and wonder how they got there. As I try to brush them off, I realize they are blood. With each breath I exhale, a fine mist of blood is spraying from my nostrils, darkening as the drops dry on the sheet. I stick my index fingers deep in my ears, and then look at the tips to see if they are bloody, too. My broken nails come out coated with dark orange ear wax and dead skin, but no blood. At least my ears haven't started bleeding yet.

I've been here before. The bed is near a window overlooking the front entrance. I glance out through the bars and see a large expanse of bleak horizon. The hospital, with its extensive grounds, stands in the middle of nowhere on the flat plains of Illinois. Rows of carefully planted trees march along the front driveway, the wind shaking their bare branches, scratching the grey dawn. Circles of hard packed earth surround the trees, and gusts swirl dry leaves between the tree trunks. As I watch them, I think of rodents traveling in packs. In the distance, I can see stalks of beige corn-stubble like giant, broken teeth protruding from the fields beyond the fence. Like my body, everything is dying. There is no warmth in any of it.

I know that bad marriages mirror late autumn in Northern Illinois. One cold, dreary day follows another; and the signs of death and decay are littered all around. The sharp, white days of winter have not begun; and early autumn, with its burst of colors, is forgotten.

At home, each of my mornings begins with anxiety. I always hope, through my actions, I can rekindle the few good days we had together. Memories of the past seduce me into believing that if I'm patient, try harder and please him, I can keep Harry from becoming angry. I forget that relationships do not follow the rhythms of the seasons. Like a fool, I think that love will reawaken, burst forth and flourish, that I will finally get everything right. I might as well try to control the weather.

* * *

The door to my hospital room opens, bringing in both noises from the corridor and a nurse. She chirps at me in her sing-song voice as if to a child.

"You're awake," she says." It's time to check your temperature."

"I'm hemorrhaging," I answer." You need to change my pads. Even my nose is bleeding," I sigh. "Look, they had to bandage my wrists." Holding up my hands, I show her the thick white bandage bracelets.

Her perfectly painted, red lips tighten; and silently, she lifts the sheet and then my gown. Her hand presses on my abdomen; and I can feel the warm blood bubble out between my legs, a spring breaking through my body's crust.

"You look much better this morning. I'll clean you now," she coos. "You'll have breakfast soon. When you're stronger, they'll start the treatment."

She uses cold tap water to wash between my legs and I stiffen and flinch, staring at the ceiling. It is rough and uneven. I try to decide if the cracks there make a map of India. I was good in geography once.

"The ceiling is a map of India," I tell her.

She stares at me for a moment and smiles." You'll be all right," she says as she turns to leave. "The treatment has helped a lot of others here, and it will help you." She stresses her last phrase and smiles again as she closes the door.

She has left the morning newspaper folded on the night stand, and I pick it up. The headline covers almost half the page. "ROSENBERGS EXECUTED," it says in thick black type. Underneath, there is a photograph of them on their way to court. Of course, I know, court is over for them now. It's just a photo the paper had on file. I look at Ethel and my stomach lurches. A small felt hat is perched on her head, its brim folded back from her face. The brim has a decoration, a round pin with a feather protruding from it at a jaunty angle. It is like my hat at home; and seeing that pale, worn face under the brim, for a moment, I think I'm looking at myself.

"We have more then just the hat in common," I say to her."I'm beginning to realize we have a life in common. I, myself, never wear shorts any longer, no matter how hot the weather. It's all because I once couldn't iron shirts right."

* * *

As a new bride, I remember standing over the ironing board, the electric fan blowing hot air into my face, sweat trickling down my collar bone to a stream between my breasts. Rosemary Clooney sings on the radio, and I sprinkle water from a bottle to soften the starch on his shirts. I look up as Harry slams the screen door and comes in shouting, "Look what those collars have done to my neck!" He moves his collar back and I see a long, chaffed, red mark.

"Oh, I haven't learned to mix the starch right yet," I laugh, nervously. "Maybe we should send the shirts to the laundry."

"You think it's funny..." Suddenly, he knocks me to the floor and the hot iron flies through the air, landing on my thigh. I scream in pain. Later, Harry tells me he never meant for it to land there, that I shouldn't aggravate him into losing his temper. I apologize.

My life has been one long apology. I've always been sorry that mother had to raise us alone, that Carol spent her childhood caring for me. I even regularly apologize to Doctor Moore because I'm so clumsy. He has to mend my broken bones too often. The doctor and Harry are friends, so he asks no questions, and wants no answers. Yes, Ethel and I keep our secrets. We both understand the deception that has filled our lives. I skim the newspaper article, but everything written there I know already.

"Your brother testified against you," I say to her. "You must remember it was to his advantage; but still, it's hard when family turns against you."

There was a time I tried to talk to Carol. She's always believed I'm the lucky one. We were sitting on the swings under the apple tree, just like young girls. I sat off center so the bandage on my thigh could not rub against the wooden seat.

Carol eyes my leg and says, "Maryanne, how could you drop..."

"It wasn't like that at all," I begin, and as I try to explain, she interrupts.
"Don't mess this up." Her mouth is tight, and the words hiss out. "You were lucky to make a good marriage." She tosses her head and dismisses me. "Can't you even iron his shirts right?"

Harry is the bank vice-president now; but everyone in town knows Carol and I were raised in the trailer park by a mother who spent her life looking for the right man. She never found him, but managed to raise hell, and us, as she sampled a legion of men in her search. I should be more grateful, but I wonder why Harry married me. He took me into his world of raised-ranch houses, Sunday brunches after church, and whispered indiscretions. Everyone pretends not to care who I am but, also, never lets me forget. My life is defined by my secrets.

"I drink in the afternoon," I tell Ethel. "Of course, it gives Harry a lot of sympathy to have a wife like me. So what if he loses his temper occasionally? Most people say it's what I deserve."

* * *

I look at the newspaper again. "Did they tell you it was electroconvulsive therapy?" I ask her.

The face in the photo stares blankly ahead. She must be stoic, like me. Did her body shutter and twist, like mine, as the jolts of electricity entered her flesh?

"Did they strap you down, so you wouldn't break your bones?" I ask. She still doesn't answer.

"They told Harry it usually works," I explain, "that, afterward, I would be happy with my life; but it didn't work the first time for me."

Then I whisper, "You have to be careful. They could kill you with their treatment."

Her expression doesn't change. She isn't the least bit interested in my secrets. Of course, I realize it's because she's dead, and I begin to laugh. As I laugh, tears roll from my eyes and my nose pours blood. I can hear the staff running to the door. They will bring an injection and I will sleep. My world will blur, softening the lines of reality, preparing me to live through the perpetual dark autumn of my life.

White Lady by Marsha J. Stried

I am saddened by the young African American men,
Who wear T-shirts bearing the message,
"No White Lady, I don't want your purse!"

Unfortunately, we as women,
Not just white women, but women of all colors,
Are forced to fear all men equally.

My fear is not based on race, color, or creed.
My fear is based on "the Land of the Free,"
Freedom to rape, rob and murder with little consequence.

And the "Home of the Brave,"
Men brave enough to not fear
our screams, tears and testimonies.

You see, I do not fear you because you are black and I am
        white.
I fear you because you are man and I am woman.

The Flight of Mrs. Hank Wallace by Stacey Thoyre

Mrs. Hank Wallace sat on a park bench and watched the river running past her. The water, the old woman thought, was the color of rotten teeth, and the aseptic October sun reminded her of the bright, cold light of hospitals. But then, most things reminded her of death, dying, or hospitals, and those things tired her. So she sat, watching the river, a black shawl snugged around her thick shoulders.

She sat a long time.

For months, she'd sat on a chair with no arm rests in her husband's hospital room. He'd lain there, unconscious, for 93 days, and Mrs. Hank Wallace had sat there, placid, for all of them. Every eight days, she'd clipped his yellowed nails, and every Sunday morning she'd asked God how long. Now, on the park bench, she sat until she was sure every ounce of water she'd first seen that morning was long gone, washed far downstream, far from sight.

The breeze that had barely ruffled the hem of her dark skirt when she arrived picked up mid-day and helped move the water. It white-capped the waves and blew a hairsprayed curl into her mouth. Her hair tasted like an old penny.

Across the river, on the opposite bank, sat two young lovers. The river, though not wide, was wide enough that the old woman could not judge the faces of the couple. A wicker basket lay on a large yellow cloth. The lovers, their plates pushed aside and a candelabra steadied in the grass beside them, sat beneath an old oak, the girl between the legs of the young man. They looked at the river or perhaps at the old woman. She could not tell.

Mrs. Hank Wallace become vaguely aware that her sitting was no longer comfortable. She felt a wriggling, a maddening crawl begin in her right buttock and zigzag down the back of her thigh. She felt her throat tighten and sweat trickle from her underarms, stopped by the thick band of underwired brassiere. This sudden bout of discomfort alarmed her. She considered herself an accomplished sitter, able to sit completely still for hours, even days, and comfortable with the way the mind drifts when the body is held down.

The girl across the river turned towards her lover, and the old woman thought she might be smiling. She shifted forward as though a few more inches might make the girl's expression less ambiguous. The girl moved again, first closer to the young man, then away. He crossed his arms lightly over his lover's shoulders, so lightly that his touch might be mistaken for the shadowed crossing of the oak's limbs. Now the young man was smiling, too, and the old woman imagined he whispered something to the girl that they found equally amusing and that his laugh did not drown out hers.

It was nearly two when a white-haired man with a black cane sat down beside her. At first, he'd thought the old woman was asleep because she sat so still. He said nothing, therefore, as he threw bread crusts to the ducks that waddled up from shore. But when his sack of crusts was nearly empty, he saw her hand reach up and remove a piece of hair that had blown into her mouth. He cleared his throat and said in a voice that made her think of plush pile carpet, "Bonjour, Madame. My name is Frederic Lacroix."

"My name is Mrs. Hank Wallace," Mrs. Hank Wallace said without inflection.

"Enchanté," he replied with a slight nod, extending his paper sack. Its serrated edge crackled in the wind. "May I offer you the last of these crusts for our web-footed friends?"

Mrs. Hank Wallace appeared dazed. She'd responded to his earlier introduction out of habit and without thought, unaccustomed to conversation. She looked at the ducks. They were quacking and scrabbling for the bits of bread.

"No," she stammered. "No, thank you." She watched as one drake charged the others, creating an open space before him. He stabbed at the sparse grass and tore up tiny clumps. Mrs. Hank Wallace noticed that the nail on the end of his bill was larger than the others' and was stained a rusty orange color. She stared at his face, judging his eyes too close together, his look narrow and spiteful. The old woman blinked twice, hard, startled by the familiarity of the bird's countenance. Hank. She blinked again, and the drake advanced towards her, quacking madly. She drew her square-heeled shoes in tightly and kept her knees locked together.

Frederic Lacroix chuckled. "Do not worry, Madame. He is just hungry. They will migrate soon." He kept the bag poised towards her.

He was still smiling when she turned to him. Sunlight flashed on his gold tooth and made her squint. She felt herself perspiring again. He'd said something to her that she could no longer remember. Her mouth was unbearably dry. Flustered, she stared at him, at his wavy white hair peeking out from under his gray cap, at the curved ends of his white moustache wagging in the wind, and at his skin, luminous in the sterile light.

Sometimes, in the 37 years before his stroke, Mr. Hank Wallace said nothing when she spoke to him. Instead, he'd cock his jaw and give her a sour look that struck her down without striking. Always, she felt her blush, and she'd swallow, swallow, swallow until the words were somewhere under her breastbone, hot and heavy enough to hump her back. When she'd caught a glimpse of herself in the dusty windows of the grocery store, she thought she looked like a question mark, and always looked away, quickly, because she couldn't bear the question her body was asking her.

"Well, Madame?" Frederic Lacroix offered one last time.

"I don't want any," she said beseechingly, as though he'd been peddling a vacuum cleaner with a vigorous beater brush.

Frederic Lacroix withdrew his sack, leaning towards the ducks.

Beneath their yellow cloth, the young couple made love.

And beside the river, Frederic Lacroix smiled as he tossed the remaining crusts to the hungry ducks. Smiling still, he stood and brushed a few crumbs that lingered on his wool slacks. The ducks quacked and rushed back to shore.

"Madame," he said again, with a note of finality.

Mrs. Hank Wallace turned and watched as he walked away, to her left, upstream. She looked again at the opposite shore but the lovers, too, had gone. Perhaps it was time for her to leave as well.

The two-lane bridge she would have to cross was on her left, less than a quarter of a mile from where she sat. She'd never walked over the bridge, though she could see there was a sidewalk on both sides for pedestrians. The cracked, black patent-leather handbag she'd been clutching to her belly burned her fingers when she opened the clasp. She pulled out the crisp, business-sized envelope that the lawyer had given her when he'd finished reading her husband's will. She held it daintily, by a corner, as though it were a photograph she didn't want to smudge. Inside the envelope was a key; while she turned the envelope, it slid into the right corner. Startled by the sudden movement, as though there might be something living inside, the old woman snatched a nail file from her handbag and slit the weighted side. The key dropped into her sweaty palm. It felt cold and heavy for its size, but not special. Its sharp tang did not thrill her. She felt no tingling along her neck, no goosebumps on her arms.

The key was rather small, really, and plain. Worse, it was ordinary, and it was then that Mrs. Hank Wallace realized how much she'd been counting on that key to transform her. It was a foolish thought, she knew, and had she known she'd been expecting so much, would have chastised herself. Set herself straight. In the open air, in front of all that moving water, in the midst of cawing birds and falling leaves, it was all so clear: the key was just a key, had always been just a key that opened nothing more than a 5 x 12 box at the bank. But she'd done all her thinking before that moment in the dark, deep within herself, where it was quiet and unmarked by the physical world. The only thing special about the key was that it had been a secret kept from her all those wedded years.

The lawyer had said the box was hers now, and the contents would ensure that her life needn't change. But didn't he know, as he surely must, that her life had already changed? That she would have never known of the box and its contents had things not changed?

She didn't care, of course, what the box contained. It had been the key that had prompted her as far as the park bench. And now, holding it in her palm, she considered turning back. Perhaps whatever change was in store for her had already happened. Perhaps she was already transformed.

For the last time, she looked at the bridge and imagined accepting the Frenchman's crusts of bread. She imagined herself smiling. She even imagined herself raising her hand towards the paper bag, but when she tried to speak, there were no sounds. Her open mouth, but not a sound. Mrs. Hank Wallace felt a familiar tightening in her chest growing into a familiar weight that curved her spine. Even in her imagination, she had no voice.

A diving shadow from a bird's wing span passed over her, and she thought at once: *Vulture.*

But it was, in fact, a sparrow, its brown speckled body alighting on a piece of driftwood in the shallows. She watched as the tiny bird pecked in the crevices of the wood, searching for sustenance. The bird, sensing her watchfulness, paused its pecking and eyed her unabashedly. The old woman stared back, seeing nothing menacing in the sparrow's lined face. After a moment, the bird returned to its pecking, but finding nothing to sustain it, flew away. The old woman, her chin thrust forward and hands fisted, followed the bird's flight towards the setting sun until it was lost in the fierce light.

Dazzled, she returned her attention to the river. It was then, her vision peppered with flash-spots, that Mrs. Hank Wallace found herself in the fleeting divine of clarity. She felt light-headed and steadied herself on the rusted rail of the bench. Trembling, she turned the key end for end, end for end. She closed her fingers around it as she looked again at the water rushing by, carrying away its contents swiftly and anonymously.

Slowly, her eyes still on the river, she uncurled her fingers. The key felt like nothing in her hand, warmed as it was from her palm; and light as it was, it barely made a sound as she slid it into her open purse. She shook her head as she snapped closed the clasp, and then she stood. Her knees, at first wobbling, held firm. She turned, upstream, towards the bridge, towards the local bank that guarded the entrance to the downtown. The wind blew the hair from her face and watered her eyes. With the strap of her handbag clutched in her hand, she started walking. When she was halfway over the bridge she looked out over the water, which seemed no longer rushing by her, but rather she by it, and felt a fine spray on her thin lips. And as she looked back at the distant place where she'd sat, Dorothy Wallace heard a small chirp and knew from the strain in her jaw that it came from her own throat.

A Free Spirit
by Joan Unterberg

"It's all mine now," she reflected. "I still can't believe that Aunt Rose and Uncle Mike left this place to me." Pouring herself a gin and tonic, Stella plopped herself in the same rickety swing that had hung between two maple trees since she was a young girl. The branches sagged and creaked under her bulky weight.

"God, it's hot. Why didn't I just sell this old place and get the hell out of the Midwest? Every summer I roast and every winter I freeze." She took a swig of her drink. "I could have used the money to travel. What's there to see around here? Flat land, corn and cows. Nothing ever happens. Nothing ever changes." She watched her cat, Maggie, wait for a grasshopper to jump from a clump of chickweed and sighed, "Even the grasshopper looks bored."

"Well, Maggie," Stella said, "at least we have a place of our own now. Forty years and the house still looks the same. I'm glad they finally installed indoor plumbing! See over there, Maggie? That's where the outhouse was. Sitting in that cold outhouse in the dead of winter was like sitting in a damned refrigerator." She mopped her brow. "I could sure use some of that cold right now. Maybe it's cooler in the cellar. Let's see what's down there."

They went into the house. Stella grabbed a flashlight and opened the heavy trap door next to the kitchen. "Be careful, Maggie. These steps are steep and slippery." Shining the light on the floor, she mumbled, "What a mess!" She kicked aside old tobacco tins and rusty beer cans and hauled several boxes upstairs. Stella shook her head as she sorted through the boxes. "Just more junk to throw away." She opened the last box and found several old bottles caked with dust and grime. When she vigorously rubbed the first bottle to see what it was, Stella's face lit up. "Why, it's a gin bottle! I wonder if there's any gin left." She quickly removed the cork.

Suddenly, a thundering, whirling, twirling funnel roared from the bottle with such force that the walls shook, pots and pans rattled, and pictures fell from the wall. Stella's eyes popped and Maggie's fur stood on end. Within seconds, the whirling dervish formed a burly hunk of a man.

"Jesus, Mary and Joseph," she gasped, "a *genie!*"

"No, my good woman, *NOT* `Jeannie!' `Harry.'"

Stella's mouth hung open, gaping at the vision in front of her. He must have stood well over six feet weighing at least two hundred pounds, all solid muscle. He was wearing a black tunic uniform coat bordered in red with a red outline of a crown on his chest. "Good Lord," she thought, "he looks just like the Beefeater on the gin bottles. He even has a beard like the man in the picture."

Finding her voice, she stammered, "Why are you here? How did you get in the bottle? Why did you get in the bottle?"

"I, my good woman, am a spirit. As a living being, I sought adventure. As a spirit, I still seek adventure and have been hopping from jug to jug, from bottle to bottle as a means of transportation. However, it does have its drawbacks. I've been sitting in that damp cellar for God knows how long and am extremely chilled. Might you have something brewing on the hearth that could warm me?"

"Hearth?" Stella asked. "Do you mean my stove?"

"I know not what you speak of, but if that is something that can chase my chills, I would be beholden to you," he replied.

Stella reached in the cupboard for a giant can of beef stew. Her hands trembled as she opened the can with her electric opener. She poured the contents on to a plate and put it in the microwave. Harry stared in amazement at the little box with a magic candle that had no flames.

Stella poured herself another gin and tonic and sat wide-eyed watching Harry contentedly devour the stew sopping up the gravy with several slices of her homemade bread. Hardly coming up for air, Harry said, "Madam, never before have I tasted such delightful food."

"Then you're sure to like this!" She handed him a slice of warm apple pie topped with three heaping scoops of vanilla ice cream.

Wiping his mouth with his sleeve, he said, "This, milady, has been a feast that King Henry himself would have relished."

"King Henry?" she asked.

"Henry the Eighth," he said. "Perhaps you have heard of him?"

"Sure," said Stella, "didn't he kill all his wives?"

"Not *all*," Harry replied, "only two. Pity," he sighed. "Anne Boleyn and Catherine Howard were quite lovely. But the king said they were both unfaithful and chop, chop, off came their heads.

"I know," he boasted, "about all the executions that took place there in the Tower of London. I was the Chief Warder. The bravest nobleman to meet his death was Sir Walter Raleigh."

"I've heard of him," Stella said. "Didn't he put his cloak over a puddle so the queen could walk on it?"

"I know not of this act of chivalry," he replied. "However, I do know that he was unjustly sentenced to death in spite of all his accomplishments."

"Why?" Stella asked.

"He disobeyed his orders. When he was sent to South America in search of gold, he was ordered not to fight the Spaniards. But Raleigh's party met a band of Spaniards and fought them.

"How well I remember the morning of his execution," Harry sighed. "Sir Walter first addressed the crowd. Then he tested the axe to make certain of its sharpness. Refusing to be blindfolded, he told the headsman, 'What dost thou fear? Strike, man, strike!'"

Although Stella seemed spellbound, she listened with her ears, not with her mind. She was far more interested in Harry's deep brown eyes than in history. She daydreamed, "What have *I* ever seen? What have *I* ever done?"

They talked far into the night. Stella told Harry, "After I lost my job, I inherited this old house and moved here from Chicago."

"Chicago?" Harry questioned.

"A city, big like London," she replied.

"Tell me about *Chicago*," he said. Stella described the city telling him about today's world using words Harry never heard before. *Planes, automobiles, trains, machines, computers, televisions, high rises.* "I am eager to behold these marvels."

Stella smiled. Her eyes wandered from his bushy brows to his mighty neck and shoulders. The fire raged in her cheeks and she longed to touch him. Her body quivering with excitement, she rose from her chair. Maggie was quietly napping near her feet.

Stella tripped over her and toppled over backwards crashing spread eagled into Maggie's kitty litter box. Maggie screeched, "Meeeowww," and ran for her life.

Jumping to the rescue, Harry asked, "Are you quite all right, Madam? That was indeed a nasty fall!"

Harry struggled to pull Stella to her feet. She held his arm tightly with one hand and flicked kitty litter from her behind with the other. Finally, she wrapped both arms tenderly around his neck pleading, "Harry, I want adventure, too. Please, take me with you."

"My dear lady, I would not know how to go about it."

She stroked his beard lovingly and stammered, "It's so boring here. I want to see the world with you."

"Methinks that perhaps you have had too much gin and are not thinking rationally."

"Harry, my mind is clear."

"But what would become of your cat?"

"The little girl next door loves Maggie. I know she'd take her in. Please, Harry, please let me go with you."

Harry looked into Stella's imploring eyes, gently touched her flushed cheeks and kissed her tenderly on her eager lips.

"And so you shall have your wish my love." Ever so slowly he moved his huge hands to her neck.

When Stella felt his fingers press against her throat, her eyes grew wide with terror. She punched him with all her might and tried to knock him to the floor. Harry didn't flinch. In desperation, she kneed him in his groin. He didn't blink. "I can't hurt him," she realized, "He's a ghost."

Harry clamped her throat like a vice until he squeezed the breath from her body.

Stella's spirit rose. "Harry, that hurt! Why did you kill me?"

"Sorry, dear lady, that was the only way I could think of to grant your request."

"Well, I guess it was worth it, if we can be together."

"To start your adventure, you must now let your spirit flow into the bottle."

Stella's spirit looked at her lifeless remains spread over the kitchen floor and then looked at the bottle. "Maybe we need a bigger bottle?" She said.

"Not really," he replied.

"Well, okay, but follow me right away!"

Stella's corpulent spirit whirled and twirled itself into the bottle. She could hardly wait for Harry to join her.

"Hurry, Harry," her hollow voice called from within the bottle.

Harry quickly grabbed the bottle. The sudden jolt threw Stella against the side. She looked upward to see if Harry was following her.

"My God, he's putting the cork in. Harry, Harry, don't!" She pleaded. "Please don't!"

"Perhaps one day I will return," he whispered. "Right now, I do not choose companionship. Furthermore, I prefer not to be confined to a bottle with someone who smells like cat shit! Cheerio, my love."

Stella's broken spirit felt Harry gently place the bottle on the mantle. Sadly, she watched him walk out into the sultry summer night.

The Lighthouse Keeper's Wife
(Door County, Wisconsin, 1855) by Constance Vogel

She polished time away
like tarnish on the wedding silver,
shined the wide oak floors befitting
the keeper's station.
When her work was done
she watched ships pass,
distant as planets,
from the narrow keyhole windows,
wished she could follow
like a gull toward the sea.
A bride of seventeen,
she found a drowned young sailor
limp as seaweed on the rocks,
remembers still his blue milk stare.

Evenings, she craved music,
begged the keeper for a piano.
So grand it wouldn't fit through the doors,
he sent it back
in the cold oatmeal dawn cradled on a barge.
Another year till a spinet came.
By day she composed lullabies
as if she had a child,
by night a dirge for the sailor
with the blue milk stare.

Replaced by a beacon the keeper
took her down the peninsula to town,
neighbors so close she could see seams on laundry.
From their porch the keeper kept watch
for children who never skinned their knees,
horses that never went lame,
asked her to play a tune sometimes,
but she never would.

Ice Fishing
by Robin Wright

At six a.m. when the alarm went off, Penelope groaned and pulled the cover up tighter around her head. Even though her body was warm, her nose still out in the air felt frozen. She imagined herself stepping on the icy floor boards and shivered. She was just dozing off when Jack called from the bathroom.

"Penelope, get up. I don't want to be late again. The expressway's going to be awful. It snowed all night and it's still coming down. I have to dig out the car, and you've got to get up now. I have a breakfast meeting, and can't be late."

God, he's so irritable all the time, she thought. Irritable or silent. Self absorbed. Full of his trouble with the board and the new artistic director and fund raising and the cut in government money and on and on. I'm so sick of this. Sleeping in the bed with that invisible line between us.

"Pen, God damn it, get up."

"I'm up, I'm up," she said, not looking at him standing in the bathroom doorway. If I get near him, I'll slug him. Maybe I should take the train, but then I'd have to walk that long, cold ten blocks to Orchestra Hall. Forget it.

Penelope flipped through the clothes in her closet and pulled out a pair of heavy, wool pants and a turtle neck and matching top sweater.

"Oh, God, I hate winter," she muttered to her reflection in the mirror. "Why am I here talking about how cold it is? Twelve years ago I said I would get out of Chicago and move to California. What happened?" she asked herself, as she wiggled and twisted into her clothes. Layers. Layers keep you warm in the cold. Just like layers of anger and resentment keep away the cold of a dead marriage. A poetic image for a failed relationship created standing partly naked in a freezing closet to avoid the hostile gaze of an old lover turned husband. It's too early in the morning to be thinking ironically. I just want to know how to get from the house to the car without going outside.

The wind howled and the snow swirled beyond the bedroom window, falling heavily, wet-blanketing the front garden and obliterating sidewalk, dead grass and street. Two car tracks marked the passage of another early riser. Penelope shivered and turned from the window. The bed with its twisted sheets, the comforter falling onto the floor, put her in mind of the last time they had made love, a long time before, it seemed now. Their embrace had been deep and warm; she had felt all the dangers to their love lay outside, somewhere far away. Now, her feet feeling the chilly floor even through her wool socks, she knew she had it wrong.

She decided not to make coffee. She would sleep in the car and get coffee downtown. She struggled into her sheepskin coat and heavy, square-toed boots, pulled her knit hat and scarf about her, and, grabbing her violin case, ran down the stairs. Shit, shit, shit, she groaned as she pulled open the door and stared at the swirling snow. She dashed across the driveway and jumped in, and they eased onto the street stretching out beneath trees drooping under their white burden.

The radio announcer droned how bad all the roads were, "Traffic is snarled and moving very slowly. Allow extra time and be cautious."

She closed her eyes and settled back into the seat already warm from the heater and thought about the cadenza she was reworking for her next recital, but as she reviewed the notes in her mind, her conversation the day before with the new assistant conductor shoved its unwelcomed way in. He had asked her how to approach Jack concerning the new budget; at the last board meeting, Jack's anger had erupted, stalling any progress for that day. Penelope remembered feeling torn, embarrassed and sorry for Jack, yet angry she was being asked to explain his behavior to a colleague. Talking to her husband would only plunge them into the unspoken rage and disappointment that lay between them. Feeling how tired she was, Penelope let her mind go limp and dozed off.

The 20 minute drive took over an hour so it was nearly 7:30 when they turned off the expressway onto the Outer Drive that ran past Lake Michigan. She opened her eyes on the frozen expanse of water and stared at the harbor just a short time before filled with boats floating in the heat, fishermen lining the banks. One of them had been Jack. He loved to fish, had loved it since he first sat on the pier and held the pole while his father baited the hook, his father, that austere old man. It was funny how little difference her knowledge of him made. As she sorted through the images of their time together, she realized she really did understand him, but somehow it didn't soften their trouble. One picture from their courtship shone so vividly.

* * *

Very early in spring when Chicago still lay frozen, they had driven south and found the sun in a blooming park in southern Illinois. In a canoe, they gilded around the deserted lake, the setting sun falling through green leaves of trees already full. They sat in companionable silence, pulled off in an inlet where the fish would lurk, and Jack had thrown his line repeatedly, changing lures with slow and deliberate precision. As she watched, wishing she had her violin to play the melody humming in her head, she thought the scene primordial. She knew she was observing a ritual so central to his being, he would always need to do it.

After a while, Jack set his pole in the bottom of the boat and paddled them around. They glided effortlessly, stopping every now and again for him to throw in his line, and they sang songs, old ones from the sixties and folk songs Jack had once played on the guitar before he'd torn off his finger trying to stuff the basketball. His wedding ring had caught on one of the metal edges of the hoop, leaving his finger dangling from the nerve – stretched almost to the breaking point.

Her efforts to pull him into her world had failed. At first, she cajoled him to concerts and plays, and he enjoyed them all, liked especially their conversation afterwards, but mostly he preferred a movie on a Friday night with beer and pizza afterwards. Music for him was his business, he argued, the way he earned his living, not the way he lived. Could it be so simple, she asked herself? Is it only that we are thoroughly mismatched?

One afternoon she had rushed off to get some small, essential ingredient for a dish he was cooking. When she returned after a half hour from a ten minute trip, in irritation he demanded, "What took you so long? This thing is nearly ruined." When she explained she had been trapped in the car by the *Eroica,* he gaped, "What?"

"I mean, I got caught in the final movement. It was playing on the radio as I drove to the store. I had to stay to hear the end. Can you understand?" she asked him. He hugged her and said, "No. Not really. I love music and I'm sorry I can't play the guitar anymore, but I don't think I'll ever listen or feel the way you do about it."

She thought about how they began, that powerful merging of souls. In fact, he had focused on her in the same way he did his fishing. When she asked him, "What was all that at the beginning, the way you loved me that blocked out the world?", he answered, laughing, "Oh, I just did that to get you," and bent his gaze back on the book he had been reading.

* * *

They inched along past the harbor and the small airport on its far side flattened with snow, the traffic control tower barely visible. A road led to Adler Planetarium, a long road lined with trees right up to the marble dome floating in a moving mist so that trees, tall and etched against the gray sky and dome, rose out of the snowy fog.

Now they were almost there. Jack switched the radio from the news station with its continuous traffic reports to a country music station he sometimes listened to. Oddly, a song they had both loved in their courtship was playing – about what goes on behind closed doors when she lets her hair hang down, and turns the lights down low.

Did we really feel that way, melting into each other, she asked herself? When was that, nearly a dozen years ago, and how far we've come into silence and resentment. Rage banked. Bitter words in passing.

In spite of herself, she felt her throat tighten and tears filled her eyes. Caught between her sadness and disgust at herself for sinking into that old lost and lonely place, she willed the lump in her throat away and swallowed hard as she stared out the window at the snow covered park and frozen water beyond.

"What are you thinking?" Jack asked, his voice soft. Again, willing her pain away behind her anger, still staring across the frozen lake, she answered, "Nothing," knowing that would silence him.

In the Art Museum by Robin Wright

the title announces "Woman as
Artist," an exhibit from the Senifro tribe
of the Ivory Coast. Around the walls
pictures of women in ritual, dancing,
mourning a sister dead in childbirth
create the first wholly female space
I remember ever seeing here.

In one photo, a lone woman stands,
honored as the Bearer of the Grain;
another holds a large ceramic water
jar she doubtless carried some way.
Still another drags behind her
a large bundle of firewood, while
from her shoulder hangs a netted
gathering of pots to be sold at
a distant market place.

I learn the women of the Senifro
create a sisterhood; among themselves,
in secret sounds, a language known only
to the initiate, during ritual they ridicule
the men, especially their sexual parts
and pride, and in dance proclaim
the abuse they suffer, safe from the
punishment words would receive.

In "call and response" the poster says,
"typical of black Africa," the women drum
their stories to ease their hearts, while
on Chicago's streets I see my sisters,
arm in arm, heads turned in heart to heart:
"Girl, wait 'til I tell you the latest," their
bright hair and wild garments dancing out
rebellion and the will to live beyond
the patterns of this man's city as their
voices ring out my freedom and theirs.

❖ **Judith Arcana's** poetry has appeared in *Frontiers, Rhino, Calyx, Exit 13, Motherwork* and *Bridges;* her first collection of poetry, *Great Lakes,* will soon be published. Her stories, essays and reviews have been published in the U.S., England and Canada. Her latest book is *Grace Paley's Life Stories, A Literary Biography.* Judith, who has taught literature, writing and Women's Studies for over 30 years, has had two residencies at Ragdale on the Illinois prairie, and several workshops at Flight of the Mind in Oregon, where she resides.

❖ **Janet Baker** lives in San Diego County, California, where she is a university professor, writer and outdoorswoman. She grew up in an Iowa farm village. Although she has lived in the Sunbelt for over 20 years, Midwestern imagery persists in her work.

❖ **Donna Black** is a multi-talented artist, an actor who works in the Chicagoland area doing film, industrials and print work. "The Old Tree" is her first nationally-published story.

❖ **Kathleen Bogan** has had her writings published in *Alaska Quarterly Review, Confrontation, Seattle Review* and other literary journals. A cousin of the acclaimed poet, Louise Bogan, Kathleen has studied with Don Justice and Philip Booth, and has been a featured reader and prizewinner in the Portland Poetry Festival. Trained as an attorney, she has been a Fulbright professor of law in Berlin.

❖ **Meredith Campbell** describes herself as "a 15 year survivor of the Midwest and of Lincoln, Nebraska, football mania," after having lived on both coasts. Her previous publication credits include *Creative Woman, Backbone, Poems by Nebraska Women* and *Front Lines.* She is at work on a novel.

❖ **Cheryl Chaffin** is working toward a Master of Fine Arts degree in Creative Writing from Vermont's Goddard College. She lives in Chicago with her partner where she teaches English as a Second Language. This award-winning poet's work has appeared in *The Sun.*

❖ **Marilyn Coffey** is a nationally known, award-winning poet whose "work about an obscene house plant" ("Pricksong") won her a prestigious Pushcart Prize. Her poems have appeared in *New America Review, Manhattan Poetry Review, Aphra, 13th Moon* and other literary journals; her non-fiction has been published by *Atlantic Monthly* as a cover story. An associate professor of creative writing in Hays, Kansas, Marilyn has studied with Joan Larkin, William Packard and Beat legend Allen Ginsberg.

❖❖❖

Marilyn's poem, "The Men of Nebraska," won the top poetry prize in *Prairie Hearts'* national competition.

❖**Lyn Coffin,** a Michigan resident, is the author of two books of poetry, *Human Trappings* and *The Poetry of Wickedness,* as well as three books of translation from the Czech. One of her fictions appeared in *Best American Short Stories 1979,* edited by Joyce Carol Oates. She has also published poetry, fiction and non-fiction in many quarterlies and small magazines, and was awarded First Prize for Translation by the Academy of American Poets. She has a novel in revision and is in the beginning stages of a dissertation on the poetry of Radcliffe Squires.

❖ **Carol Cowen** was born in Chicago, graduated from Indiana University, and lives in the Bay Area, "where she feels especially comfortable." Her writings have been published in *Whole Earth Review, The Old Red Kimono* and *Noe Valley Voice.* She was named second place winner of Writer's Digest Short Story contest in 1994 and scholarship winner to Squaw Valley Writers Conference in 1995. She writes in a six-windowed studio overlooking California's largest lake, often of rural Japan, where she taught English for a year.

❖ **Jo Lee Dibert-Fitko,** writer, cartoonist and vocalist, lives in Frankenmuth, Michigan. Her work has appeared in over 75 publications. She is a featured poet, guest speaker and consultant on the healing art of humor. Her national awards include recognitions from *Mulberry Press, Zuzu's Petals, Portals,* Illinois' Rockford Art Museum and the Poetry Society of Michigan.

❖ **Sharon Dornberg-Lee** is a Chicago native living there with her husband and two cats, and is pursuing a Masters Degree in clinical social work at the University of Chicago. In 1993, she published a collection of poetry, *Before We Reach the Sky,* with three other Feminist Writers Guild members. Her *Prairie Hearts* contribution was inspired by her volunteer experience at Chicago House, a social service agency providing support for people with AIDS.

❖ **Kelly Eastern** earned her Masters Degree in Fine Arts in playwriting from the University of California, San Diego. Her plays have been performed in California, New York, and Ohio. She currently teaches at the University of North Carolina. Her work is published in *Connecticut Review, Frontiers, Midstream, N.Y.U. Review* and *Phoebe, Journal of Feminist Scholarship Theory and Aesthetics.* An earlier version of "The Scientific Theory..." titled "Winter Story," appeared in *Connecticut Review.*

❖**Carol Gloor** of Chicago earned her Bachelors and Masters Degrees in English from Roosevelt University, and her J.D. from Northwestern University. This " half-century old attorney" in private practice is the recipient of the nationally-renowned Amelia Award for short poetry. Her poems have been published in *Korone, Jane's Stories* and *River Oak Review.* She is co-author of *Before We Reach the Sky.*

❖**Barbara Govednik** is a resident of Evanston, Illinois, who writes in multiple areas - business, humor and essay - "not mutually exclusive," she notes. Her essays have been published in *Rosebud* and the *Chicago Tribune.* In 1995, Chronicle Books released her humor book *Are We There Yet and 99 Other Reasons Not to Have Kids.*

❖**Nancy Hagen** earned her degree in English literature from the University of Michigan. A newspaper reporter for several years, she has won numerous awards for her feature writing from Suburban Newspapers of America and the Maryland-Delaware-D.C. Press Association. She is now a full-time fiction writer working on short stories and a mystery novel. Currently a resident of Indiana, she has lived in several states in the Midwest.

❖**Jane Haldiman** is originally from the St. Louis area and has been "migrating northward through Illinois ever since." She has degrees from Knox College and Illinois State University, both in English and creative writing. She lives in Chicago, writes poetry and prose, and works as a proofreader. Her previous publications include pieces in *Small Press Review* and *The Waukegan Free Press.*

❖**Rose Hamilton-Gottlieb** is a native Iowan who has lived in California for many years. Her work appears in *Farm Wives and Other Iowa Stories, Room of One's Own, The Elephant Ear, Aethlon* and *Grow Old with Me the Best Is Yet To Be.* A one-time instructor of history and American Studies in the California State University and Community College systems, she now devotes all her time to writing fiction.

❖**Patricia W. Herczfeld** is a certified public accountant and president of The Aurelius Group, a financial planning firm. She earned a Master of Liberal Studies from Mundelein College and chose as her field of inquiry the relationship of art and work. Her poetry has been published in *Critical Perspectives in Accounting.* She is a life-long resident of Chicago, where she performs her poetry and fiction.

❖**Joyce Hinnefeld** is a writer, editor and teacher of writing whose work has appeared in *Farmer's Market, The Greensboro Review, 13th Moon* and other journals. She recently completed a Ph.D. in English, with a concentration in creative writing, at the State University of New York at Albany. She has worked in college publishing, taught at a variety of East Coast colleges, and has completed her first novel, *Rumer Rutledge Tells the Truth.* Born and raised in southern Indiana, she lived in Chicago for several years before moving to New York City in 1987; she now makes her home in the Hudson River valley.

❖**Jen Hinton** has read her poetry and short fiction in many book stores and performance venues in the Chicago area. Her work has been published in anthologies including *Skin Deep*, a collection of writings from women of color.

❖**Kay Jordan** is a former Iowan living and writing in Arizona. She has published fiction, feature articles, essays and poetry. In 1995 she was awarded a sistership to Norcroft, a writing retreat for women, and won the *Buffalo Bones* short story contest . Kay is currently marketing a mystery featuring a female herpetologist and working on a novel set in Iowa in 1946.

❖**Marcia Karlin** is a native Midwesterner, a multi-talented artist whose contemporary art quilts have been nationally exhibited and featured in newspapers, magazines and books. Her award-winning work hangs in many private and corporate collections. Her interest in artists' books led to a renewed exploration of language as a means of creating images and examining meaning. Her poems have won prizes sponsored by the Poets and Patrons Club of Chicago, as well as the Jo-Anne Hirshfield Memorial Poetry Awards. She has studied with Joseph Parisi, Maureen Seaton and Whitney Scott. Her work appears in *Mediphors.*

❖❖❖

Marcia's poem, "Fallen Angels," won the Outrider Press Award for best submission by a Feminist Writers Guild member.

❖**Susanna Lang** has given readings with the Feminist Writers Guild and at Cafe Voltaire in Chicago. She has published original poems and essays, and translations from the French, in such journals as *Southern Poetry Review, World Literature Today, Chicago Review, Sub-stance, New Directions* and *Green Mountain Review.* Her book publications include translations of *Words in Stone* and *The Origin of Language,* both by Yves Bonnefoy. She also teaches Humanities to middle school students in Chicago.

❖**Anne Massaro** is a former teacher in the Chicago Public Schools, holding a Masters Degree in Early Childhood Education. Her love of children and reverence for all of nature are reflected in her poetry and essays. She has published a chapbook of her poetry and read at Women's Writing Workshops and Oak Lawn Library poetry readings. She is currently working on a collection combining her haiku and watercolors. She and her husband live in Evergreen Park, Illinois.

❖**Kathy Mayer** is a full-time writer living in Indiana. Her publications include non-fiction articles in more than 50 magazines, and she is co-author with Szifra Birke of *Together We Heal* (Ballantine Books, 1990). She has won several Women in Communications regional awards, frequently leads writing workshops and reads her creative writing at the Wells Community Cultural Center in Lafayette.

❖ **Ethney McMahon** lives in Denver, Colorado, where she "pushes books for a living." She has attended the Iowa Summer Writing Workshops, and her work has appeared in *Buffalo Bones* and *Writing For Our Lives.* Since settling in Denver, Ethney has become accustomed to the altitude, "but is still learning to acclimate herself to her Muse's hours and desires."

❖**Gwyn McVay** is associate editor of *AWP Chronicle.* She grew up in North Dakota and still has family ties to the Midwest. "Hawk Season" was written on an annual cross-country trek to Iowa. Her poetry has appeared recently in *Phoebe,* the *Greensboro Review,* and *The American Voice.* Her chapbook, *Brother Ikon,* is scheduled for 1996 publication in a limited edition from Inkstone Press.

❖**Karla Linn Merrifield,** director of Marketing Communications at State University of New York College at Brockport., is completing her Masters Degree in creative writing at the College. Her poetry has most recently been published in *Negative Capability* and *Earth's Daughters;* last spring, her first chapbook appeared, *The Sweet Heart of Nature.*

❖**Lee Mirand,** current editor of the *Feminist Writers Guild Newsletter,* has been a Chicago resident for five years. Originally in the Midwest to pursue her dream of acting, she trained in comedy improv at Player's Workshop, part of Second City. However, "after realizing her stage fright was incurable," she decided to pursue her other love, writing. This is Lee's first nationally-published piece.

❖**Lydia Nowak,** a lifelong resident of Illinois, is an elementary school teacher in the City of Chicago Public School System. Her poetry has appeared in *The Cardinal* and in *Jane's Stories,* published by Wild Dove Press.

❖**Joan Shea O'Neal**, who lives in St. Louis, can usually be found either working in a laboratory or writing poetry. She is a chemist who has co-authored articles published in *The Journal of Biological Chemistry, The Journal of Medicinal Chemistry,* and *Medicinal Chemistry Research.* "Dichotomy" is her first published poem.

❖**Ann Oomen** is a poet, writer and teacher whose work has been published in state and regional journals. Her essays and poetry have won regional awards. She works as a Writer-in-Residence in Great Lakes area schools, and as Coordinator of the Writing Center at Lake Forest Academy. She is co-author of the chapbook, *Moniker* with Ray Nargis. She offers guest performances of poems and stories from the oral tradition through her program, *By Heart.* She lives with her partner and cat in Illinois.

❖**Nancy Peiffer** is a 1993 graduate of the University of Illinois at Chicago with a degree in history. Having moved to the state of Washington in 1993, she is back in Illinois on an extended writing trip pursuing family history. She plans to write children's stories, juvenile literature, short fiction and poetry based on her research. In Seattle she was published by *The Stranger, Amazon* and *Real Change.* Her poetry has appeared in *Poetry Motel* and *Rent-A-Chicken Speaks.*

❖**Mary Damon Peltier's** poems and feminist essays have been published in small magazines and anthologies. She has given poetry readings at colleges and book stores and on Boston area radio/television. Mary was co-founder of a women's newspaper in Massachusetts, *Hysteria,* and of the poetry journal *Women/Poems.* She has been a political activist, taught creative writing, and given many presentations about goddess stories and issues in social justice. Her Ph.D. studies focus on goddess mythology and alchemy. A native of New England, she first fell in love with the prairie while driving and camping cross-country with women friends in the 1970s.

❖**Laura Smith Porter** grew up in Central Illinois but now lives in Massachusetts. She has a Ph.D. in American History from Princeton University, and teaches women's history, specializing in women's autobiography. Her work appears in *Sistersong: Women Across Cultures* and *The Sun.* The idea for "I-57" came from a childhood spent traveling that highway.

❖**Rita Reinert** has been active in Chicagoland neighborhood politics for over a decade, serving as president of United Neighborhood Organization (UNO) for four years. She was an election judge in the 15th Ward for eight years and has worked extensively with Danny Solis, now alderman of Chicago's 23rd Ward, creating changes in the city's police department and board of education. She is the author of *Boots - Trailing the Appalachians,* an autobiographical work recalling her Appalachian Trail hike at age 60.

❖**Mie Hae Rhee** hails from Korea and now lives in Illinois with her husband. She is an ordained minister, a Korean translator at Midwest Christian Center, and an instructor at the Midwest Campus of Oral Roberts University. She has a B.A. in Social Work from Ewha Women's University in Korea, an M.S.W. from Ohio State University, and an M.P.H. from the University of Illinois. She has worked at various social service agencies in Korea and America, and writes articles for Korean newspapers. "Tornado" is her first work in English to be published.

❖ **Kim Rinn** is a poet living in Ypsilanti, Michigan. She is published in the 1995 issue of *Northern Spies* and was a reader at the 10th anniversary celebration of the publication. She most recently read her works as part of the Arts and Events series at Washtenaw Community College, and is currently employed as a data processing manager at Ann Arbor, Michigan.

❖**Marcia Schwartz** of Los Angeles, California, is a distinguished member of the **ISP** and a member of the **ISAA**-1966. Her poetry is published in anthologies, journals and magazines. To date she has written over 300 poems, and has won a bronze medal, four blue ribbons and recognition in literary magazines. Marcia loves poetry and its power to express her thoughts in writing, believing "poetry is the true soul of the poet."

❖**Patti See,** who makes her home in Chippewa Falls, Wisconsin, has had her work published in *The Cincinnati Poets' Collective, Sun Dog: The Southeast Review, Upriver: Wisconsin Poetry and Prose, Wisconsin English Journal, Gypsy Cab,* and *Talking River Review.* As an Instructional Program Manager at the University of Wisconsin-Eau Claire, she supervises a tutoring and mentoring program for students of color and a tutoring program for students with disabilities. She also teaches developmental education courses.

❖**Jennifer Sheridan** received a Masters of Fine Arts in fiction writing from Columbia College in Chicago. Her stories have appeared in several literary publications including *Hyphen, The Best of Hair Trigger* and *Emergence.* In 1992 her writing placed first in the Columbia University Press Association Golden Circle Awards for experimental fiction. Jennifer makes her home in Chicago.

❖**Joan Shroyer-Keno** is a 1980 journalism graduate of Kent State University in Ohio and has written poetry since grade school. She grew up in Ohio and has lived in Mississippi and Wisconsin. Her poems have appeared in various publications throughout the United States. Her work placed fourth in the 1994 Virginia Highlands Literature Festival, and in 1995 also placed fourth in the Coos Bay/Mary Scheirman Poetry Award in Coos Bay, Oregon. In free moments, she enjoys "being close to the earth via gardening and listening to her inner voice of inspiration." She resides in Knoxville, Tennessee, with her husband and three cats.

❖**Kelly Sievers** grew up in Milwaukee, Wisconsin, and went to nursing school in Rochester, Minnesota. She now works full-time as a nurse anesthetist in Oregon. Her poetry has been published in *Ellipsis, The Seattle Review, Writer's Forum, Hayden's Ferry Review, Descant, Calapooya Collage, Poet and Critic, The Bridge,* and *Fireweed.* Kelly's latest poems are forthcoming in *The Seattle Review, Fireweed* and *Prairie Schooner.* "Samples" appeared previously in the Winter 1989-90 issue of *The Greensboro Review.* Her award-winning chapbook is entitled *Making Room,* and was published in 1995 by Alsi Press.

❖**Claudia Rosa Silva** describes herself as "a 19 year old, Mexican, bilingual, Latina poet who resides in the downtown Chicago area." Currently studying at the University of Illinois at Chicago, she has been writing poetry for four years, participating in creative writing workshops and crafting her skills by working one-on-one with a Chicagoland poet for the past three years. Her work appears in literary journals including *Edda* and *Dividends*. Claudia has performed with other Feminist Writers Guild members and feels "There is nothing more special to me than creating and sharing through words."

❖**Margie Skelly** is a well known Chicago poet, the recipient of three Poets and Patrons awards. She has also been awarded the Lila Wallace grant for poetry in conjunction with Poets and Writers, Inc., performing at WomanMade Gallery. An Illinois Artist in Residence finalist in fiction and poetry, she co-authored *Before We Reach the Sky,* a collection of poetry by four feminist writers. Her work has been published in many literary journals and magazines including *Korone, Black Maria, Primavera* and *Rambunctious Review.*

❖ **Grazina Smith's** short story, "The Road to Recovery," is her first appearance in print. A member of the Feminist Writers Guild, she has participated in readings at Waterstone's Book sellers on North Michigan Avenue. She has performed her work at St. Xavier University and at readings sponsored by the University of Chicago.

❖**Marsha Stried** is working on her first novel. She graduated from the University of Illinois with a Speech Communication degree. She writes, "My memberships in groups such as the Feminist Writers Guild, the National Organization for Women and the Illinois Democratic Party have given me the opportunity to stay abreast of the issues facing women today." In fall, 1996 she will begin the Masters program in Women's Studies at DePaul University.

❖ **Stacey Thoyre** grew up in Stevens Point, Wisconsin, and lives in San Francisco with her husband and two cats. She received her undergraduate degree in business from the University of Wisconsin and went on to earn a Masters of Arts in Creative Writing from the University of San Francisco in 1993. She has recently completed her first collection of short stories, *The Magnificent Electric Lost Memory Parade & Other Stories.* Stacey designs and makes stained glass windows, likening the process of balancing color, texture and line to the structuring of fiction. She believes in the organic quality of fiction, grow ing her characters "out of thin air, in Mrs. Hank Wallace's case, a park bench."

❖❖❖

"The Flight of Mrs. Hank Wallace" won the top fiction prize in *Prairie Hearts'* national competition.

❖**Joan Unterberg** was born and raised in Chicago. After their three children were born, Joan and her husband became spies for the CIA, working for the covert branch in Antarctica. After several close calls with polar bears, she quit the CIA and became lead vocalist for the Magyar Gypsy Band, playing for weddings, funerals and bar mitzvahs in Hungary. Eventually she performed at a number of high level state occasions, entertaining Winston Churchill and Josef Stalin. She is now retired and pursuing her lifelong dream of writing.

❖**Constance Vogel** has published over 100 poems in literary magazines including *Spoon River Poetry Review, Korone, Blue Unicorn, Willow Review* and *Jane's Stories.* In addition to having her poems broadcast on Dial-a-Poem Chicago, she was nominated for a Pushcart Prize in 1994. Her poetry collection is titled *Caged Birds.*

❖**Robin Wright** is a professor of English and Director of Women's Studies at Harold Washington College in Chicago. She earned a Ph.D. in the Sociology of Language from the University of Chicago. She edited *Wyrd Women/Word Women,* a collection of women's writings from the Writing Workshop for Women she directed for a decade. In 1991 she was the recipient of an Illinois Arts Council Fellowship for non-fiction. Her publications include scholarly work on women's language as well as essays and short stories. She writes of her particular pride "in the many students from my classes who have been published and are pursuing advanced degrees in creative writing."

❖ **Whitney Scott** has had her poetry and fiction published from coast to coast in many literary journals including *Howling Dog, Wide Open, Potomac Review, Art & Understanding, Kaleidoscope, Tomorrow Magazine, Pearl, CQ* and others.

She teaches creative writing, recently presenting a seminar on Post Feminist Writing at DePaul University. She led the Women's Writing Workshop at St. Xavier University from 1990 to 1995 and headlined the 1992 Taste of Chicago Writers Conference there. In addition, she sits on the planning committee of Chicago's Printers Row Book Fair, the nation's third largest event of its kind.

Scott regularly reviews books for *Outlines* and *Booklist* magazine and has been featured as a guest author in the Illinois Authors Series at Chicago's Harold Washington Library.

She has studied with the internationally acclaimed writer Grace Paley, as well as with authors Carol Anshaw, Denise Chavez, Albert Goldbarth, Miriam Sagan and Elizabeth Tallent. In addition to editing the anthology *Words Against the Shifting Seasons*, Scott is author of the novel *Dancing to the End of the Shining Bar.* She is currently at work on a crime novel. Ms. Scott is represented by the Victoria Sanders Literary Agency in New York City.

End Notes

This anthology of women's writings on the Midwest is published by Outrider Press, Inc. in affiliation with the Feminist Writers Guild, whose national contest and call for manuscripts yielded these submissions. Details on the Feminist Writers Guild and its activities may be had by calling or faxing 708.672. 6630.

Every effort has been made to locate and credit any prior publications of writings in this book. If any have not been credited, please notify the Publisher so that every effort to correct this will be made in future printings.

"The Scientific Properties..." by Kelly Easton appeared with changes in *Connecticut Review*.

"Samples" by Kelly Sievers appeared in *The Greensboro Review*.

To Order Outrider Press Publications

Prairie Hearts @$14.95
   Number Ordered____ Amount . . . .

Dancing to the End of the Shining Bar @9.95
   Number Ordered____ Amount . . . .

Listen to the Moon @ 4.00
   Number Ordered____ Amount . . . .

        Illinois residents add 7.5% tax . . . .

        Add Shipping/Handling Fees
                $2.25 for any one book . . . .
                $3.25 for any two books . . . .
                $4.00 for all three . . . .

TOTAL . . . .

Mail this order form with check or money order to:

Outrider Press
1004 East Steger Road, Suite C-3
Crete, Illinois 60417